A Guide to
Inclusive Therapy

Also by Bill O'Hanlon
with W. W. Norton Professional Books

A Brief Guide to Brief Therapy (with Brian Cade)

A Guide to Possibility-Land (with Sandy Beadle)

An Uncommon Casebook (with Angela Hexum)

Even From a Broken Web (with Bob Bertolino)

In Search of Solutions (with Michele Weiner-Davis)

Stop Blaming, Start Loving (with Pat Hudson)

Rewriting Love Stories (with Pat Hudson)

Solution-Oriented Hypnosis (with Michael Martin)

Taproots

A Guide to Inclusive Therapy

· ·

26 Methods of Respectful, Resistance-Dissolving Therapy

BILL O'HANLON

W·W·NORTON

NEW YORK · LONDON

For information about permission to
reproduce selections from this book, write to
Permissions, W.W. Norton & Company, Inc.
500 Fifth Avenue, New York, NY 10110

Composition and book design by Ecomlinks, Inc.
Manufacturing by Haddon Craftsman
Production Manager: Leeann Graham

Library of Congress Cataloging-in-Publication Data
O'Hanlon, William Hudson
A guide to inclusive therapy: 26 methods of respectful, resistance-dissolving therapy/
Bill O'Hanlon
    p.   cm.
"A Norton professional book."
ISBN 0-393-70410-6 (pbk)
1. Psychotherapy—Methodology. 2. Resistance (Psychoanalysis). I. Title.
RC489.R49037/2003
616.89'14—dc21   200244485

W.W. Norton & Company, Inc., 500 Fifth Avenue, New York, NY 10110
www.wwnorton.com

W.W. Norton & Company, Ltd., Castle House, 75/76 Wells Street, London W1T 3QT

FOR STEFFANIE
Inclusiveness personified.
Thanks for having room for all of me.

Contents

A Guide to Inclusive Therapy

Introduction

Some years ago, Sandy Beadle and I wrote *A Guide to Possibility-Land: 51 Methods of Respectful Brief Therapy*. Originally intended to be a CD-ROM, it turned into a book. Sandy had studied how to make ideas memorable and easy to learn, and the book turned out to be unexpectedly popular. It was written in a fun, easily digestible manner, with whimsical drawings designed to help readers remember the key ideas. I owe Sandy a debt of gratitude for this form. Because I have tackled this one on my own, however, Sandy can't be held liable for any failures readers might find in these pages.

This book is the briefest introduction to and overview of the philosophy and methods of Inclusive Therapy that I could write. I am so excited about this way of working, which can be used by therapists of any persuasion, that I wanted to get it out in written form as quickly as possible. I also wanted to make it as accessible as possible, as I have discovered that busy therapists are more likely to read shorter, bite-sized books and chapters rather than lengthy tomes.

My original title for the book was: *There's No Such Thing as a Weed: A Little Book of Inclusive Therapy*. (The idea about weeds was borrowed from a song by the English group The Move.) But I was persuaded to change it in favor of the current title. The former title, however, reflects the sensibility basic to this book: to see the value in those things we therapists or

our clients usually think of as
annoyances or sources of resistance to successful therapy. A
quotation from the classic
American Zen book *Zen Mind,*
Beginner's Mind captures the spirit of inclusiveness well:

> For Zen students a weed, which for most people is
> worthless, is a treasure. With this attitude, whatever you
> do, life becomes an art.*

I am suggesting, following Suzuki, that this inclusive attitude—
dealing with conflicts, ambivalence, resistance, and other
"weeds" of therapy—can become an art.

I have taught this approach to thousands of therapists all over
the world. Many clinicians have told me of its effectiveness in
assisting their most challenging clients, people who have been
unresponsive or resistant to other approaches. This mode of
therapy is especially useful for people who have been diagnosed with "borderline personality disorder." Borderline
Personality Disorder seems to be characterized by a push-pull
kind of response: *You can't help; please save me. I will push you
away; please don't give up on me.* So, Inclusive Therapy, which
responds to this ambivalent and seemingly contradictory com-
munications, is ideally suited for use with borderline clients.

Foreshadowing of Inclusive Therapy

I was a serious and thoughtful young Catholic boy. When I
became a teenager, however, my faith began to crack. This crack

---

* Shunryu Suzuki (1997). *Zen Mind, Beginner's Mind* (New York & Tokyo: Wheatherhill), p. 121.

came about in part because I was studying one of the texts of Roman Catholic dogma regularly read by schoolchildren, *The Baltimore Catechism*. In the text there was a description of the nature of God. He was described as omnipresent.

Omnipresent: He is everywhere. As I pondered this, I came across a paradox I couldn't resolve. If God is everywhere, He must be in the Devil. If He is in the Devil, He must also be the Devil. How can this be? But when I asked my religion teacher, she told me, "We don't ask such questions." And that was that, at least for her. As for myself, I began to see a crack in the logic of the Roman Catholic belief system. Years later, reading Herman Hesse, I came across the notion of Abraxas, the dual-natured god. Of course, the  Romans had Janus, the two-faced god. Hindus believe in Kali, who simultaneously creates and destroys. As time went on I discovered that many cultures have dealt with this complex nature of the divine. The seeds of Inclusive Therapy, though, were planted in those teenage years of religious questioning.

(And, before I get a bunch of letters and emails from Catholics, I hasten to add that a good Jesuit could have answered my question, within the terms of Catholic dogma, very easily and well. There is nothing about deep Roman Catholicism that can't contain opposites and the complex nature of life and the divine.)

Let me tell you the story of how this approach first crystallized for me some years later.

How I Discovered Inclusive Therapy

I once treated a man named Abel who had a severe case of obsessive-compulsive disorder. Abel told me about his many intrusive obsessions. He told me he obsessed all the time. If one obsession went away, another would immediately take its place. He was, he said, symptomatic from the moment he woke up until the moment he went to sleep.

Abel had been referred to me by a friend of his who, as a client of mine, had found the hypnosis I had used to be helpful. Abel didn't believe that hypnosis would work for him because he  was so obsessive and tense. After hearing that he had tried most every other therapeutic technique, however, I suggested we give it a try. I did a bit of hypnosis in the first session, but Abel looked very uncomfortable, moving around and tensing his facial muscles throughout the process. He wasn't impressed with the initial experience, but was willing to give it another try. I assured him that we would have more time in the next session and suggested that a longer trance might yield better results.

During our next appointment, I conducted a forty-minute hypnosis session with Abel. For about fifteen minutes of that trance, Abel was symptom-free and continued to be symptom-free for about two hours afterwards. Even though he still wasn't convinced that hypnosis would work for him, and he didn't entirely believe he had been in trance, Abel was impressed and happy that something had helped. He had tried so many therapies without getting any relief from his obsessions that two hours of relief suggested some promise.

At the third session, I began again with the hypnosis.

Bill: Okay, for this trance you can keep your eyes open or you can shut them.

Abel closed his eyes, as he usually did.

Bill: And as you're sitting there, you may be thinking you are not going to be able to go into trance. You can have that thought; that's okay. You may be thinking that trance is not going to work. You can think that; that's okay. You may be distracted by one of your symptoms, maybe by the tension in your jaw or your neck. You may think you're too tense to go into trance, and that's okay. You can be tense and you can still go into trance and you might relax as the moments go on. But you don't have to relax to go into trance. You may be obsessing. You can just let yourself feel what you feel, think what you think, experience what you're experiencing, not think what you don't think, not experience what you don't experience, not feel what you don't feel, and you can continue to go into trance.

At that point Abel popped his eyes open.

Abel: That's it. Do more of that. That's what helped me last
time.

Bill: You mean do more trance?

Abel: [replying impatiently] No, no. I don't think I am going
into trance or that hypnosis will work for me. But what
you are doing now is exactly what I need. That's what
helped me last time. Do more of that.

Bill: What do you mean?

Abel: The way you are talking now. That is what is helping
me. Because somehow when you talk that way, for a
brief period of time I get the sense I can't do anything
wrong. It's the only time in my life when I can't do anything wrong. I long for that sense. So you can skip the
hypnosis, but keep saying those kinds of things, because
that's what I need.

In that moment something crystallized for me. I had been
doing just what I had done with Abel with many people. Their

inner experience, like that of Abel, was
often one of feeling that something (or
everything) they were doing was somehow wrong. Having *all* of their experience validated and included was a very
powerful intervention.

I first learned the effectiveness of an
inclusive approach from doing hypnosis
in the tradition of the late psychiatrist
Milton H. Erickson. Erickson had a very
permissive, rather than rigid, approach to helping people experience altered states. People who seek hypnosis often have
these strange and restrictive ideas about hypnosis: what it is

about; what will happen during it; or what will be required of them to enter trance. Among other things, they believe that they must be relaxed to go into trance, that they won't hear anything that the hypnotist says or any noises around them, or that they will be knocked out, completely unconscious.

None of those are essential, of course, for experiencing trance. But many people define hypnosis in these narrow terms, tightly bound by *musts* and *can'ts*. What the hypnotist has to do is make the circle bigger, take the pressure off people so that they don't have to have these experiences, or allow them to have these experiences without the feeling that they must have them.

So I say:

You don't have to be relaxed and you can relax. You can listen to or hear everything that I say or you don't have to. You may remember what I say and you may not remember. You don't have to believe anything about this.

I just start to unhook people from the necessities and the impossibilities. I remove the pressure that they put on themselves. This is done by valuing and validating everything about their experience, even the opposite of what they think they need to be doing at the moment. Perhaps they're thinking: "I need to relax. My jaws are tense." In response, the first thing I do is value that tension, value their being tense at that moment. The second thing I do is present the possibility of the tension not being there. I might say something like this:

> **You can notice the tension in your jaw, you can have tension in your jaw or your neck or your throat and you don't have to be tense. You may relax, but you don't have to relax. And you can go into trance even if you aren't relaxed.**

After my experience with Abel, I realized what I had learned from years of doing hypnosis Erickson-style. I had gone even further than Erickson had into permission and inclusion, and developed a way of working that no longer even required hypnosis or trance.

I began to call this way of working *Inclusion* or *Inclusive Therapy*.

The Powerlessness of Positive Thinking

In the mid-1980s I was involved with the development of *solution-based therapy*. I called my version *solution-oriented*. In this I was also inspired by Erickson, who almost never met a problem he couldn't solve. He was able to fer- ret out strengths and abilities in the midst of seemingly intractable pathologies. I came to write many books and articles about the approach, but something began to worry me. Sometimes people would come up to me at breaks in workshops I was teaching and say, "I really like your *positive* approach." This bothered me immensely, as I felt that it missed the essence of the approach. By the early 1990s, I was worried that many therapists had fundamentally misunderstood the approach and were only getting the "cheap" version—pure positive thinking and the mere denial of problems.

Around that time, when I began to speak publicly about this worry, a therapist named David Nylund approached me during a break in one workshop. David told me that the clinicians in his clinic had been converted to the solution-focused approach and subsequently they had begun to notice the same problem. From behind the one-way mirror, David and his fellow clinicians would watch one of their colleagues as he or she would try to get a client to stay focused on solutions and solution-talk. Many clients they observed went along and seem to benefit. Yet there were some who were frustrated by this technique and, as the session went on, became increasingly alienated. The therapist, however, would often seem oblivious to the building resentment and discomfort of these

clients as he or she continued asking about what worked, what was going better, and so on. David and his colleagues had come up with a name for this phenomenon: solution-*forced* therapy. I laughed and suggested that he write the idea up for a journal (which he later did).

What could be done about it, though?, David asked.

I told him that I had been moving away from a solution focus and talking more about inclusion. What I had been doing was a kind of mutant child of the approaches of Carl Rogers and

Erickson—acknowledging and validating people's experience, while inviting them into change and the recognition of new possibilities.

Positive thinking is like telling yourself: "Everyday in every way, things are getting better and better." Things are more complex. As I look around the world, with its violence, racism, sexism, and manifold inequities, I can't help but think things are more mixed. (Some things are getting better, some things are getting worse, and some things are staying about the same.) As I look at my clients, the same is true. Family therapist Ken Hardy expressed it well:

> Life is a messy and confusing tangle of middle ground, neither here nor there, never just black or white. I've come to believe that as important as it is for therapists to know the right intervention to end a family's emotional gridlock, its just as important to resist the pull of polarized thinking—either/or, good or evil, victim or perpetrator, pro-choice or pro-life, or any one of a million dichotomies that shape our identities and our culture. . . .*

Positive thinking is like putting a thin layer of gold foil over a pile of manure. It looks good from a distance, but, if you poke your finger at it, you quickly break through to the not so good stuff.

---

*See Hardy (1995, November/December). Embracing Both/And. *The Family Therapy Networker,* 19(6): 42–57.

Of course, negative thinking is not a viable alternative. To think negatively is just to resign oneself to the idea that life is nothing but a pile of manure. Violence, cruelty, and inequity are as old as time, one might think. Genetic and biochemical disorders abound and determine people's lives. People are abused and damaged in childhood.

People are resistant to change. That's just the way it is, the negative thinker will conclude. One of my graduate school professors proclaimed, "The only person who wants to change is a wet baby!" I knew he was wrong, because I had already worked as a paraprofessional counselor and had seen many people who not only wanted to change but *who had changed*. I had also seen others who hadn't changed despite the best efforts of friends and therapists. There were also people who were ambivalent about changing. They wanted to change, but were afraid of what changing would entail.

I once had a client come to my office and tell me that she had to kill herself. I took that seriously, of course. But in the back of my mind, I was thinking:

I don't believe you. If you were totally committed to ending your life, you would have just stayed at home and done it. The fact that you got yourself out of the house and came to my office to tell me this means that there must

be some little part of you that is not committed to dying and wants to live.

I also remember hearing about interviews of people who survived suicide attempts in which they jumped off the Golden
Gate Bridge. Most
people who jump
die. But there
were several peo-
ple over the years
who by chance
survived the fall.
Some researchers
received a grant

to study them and these researchers could not find any common factors in the lives of these attempted suicides except
that each of them reported that, on the way down, he or she
had some variation on the thought: "Hmmm. Maybe this wasn't
such a good idea." I suspect that most people who seek therapy have at least a little of the same ambivalence. It is our job
as therapists to recognize the suicidal impulse as well as the
desire to live or, at least, the doubt about dying.

What I am pointing to by proposing this inclusive approach is
that we must face pain, suffering, problems, and inequity even
while we step into the possibility that things can be different.
The best stance in the face of such complexity is to acknowl-
edge the problems and at the same time to recognize the possibility for change.

In the movie *What Dreams May Come*, Robin Williams's character must leave Heaven and descend into Hell in order to res-

cue his wife. In doing so, he almost gets stuck with her in *her* Hell, as he must join her in her vision of Hell and almost gets lost in that horrific vision. But Williams's character is finally able to remember something beyond Hell, and this recollection saves them both. Similarly, in the song "Trouble," Shawn Colvin sings about staying connected with her partner when he is depressed:

> I go to the trouble like a light or like a ... friend. ... You
> don't have to drag me down, I descend.

I think in these two examples we find the essence of good therapy. To be able to descend with people into their Hell and yet keep one foot in possibility-land.

Recognize that there is a pile of manure so you don't step in it inadvertently—then clean it up or use it as compost.

The Power of Inclusive Thinking

I have found that for people suffering from complex dissociative and posttraumatic stress problems, as well as people diagnosed with borderline personality disorder, Inclusive Therapy is very effective. Why? Because it recognizes the complex and contradictory feelings they experience and the equally mixed messages they communicate to others.

I was in the midst of a difficult treatment with Kim, who had been severely and persistently abused as a child. She lived about a 6-hour drive away from me and we met every month or so for long sessions of three hours. Between the matter and length of our sessions, the work we were doing was leaving Kim emotionally raw. She called one day and told me she couldn't go on with the therapy. I knew by now that Kim struggled with suicidal impulses for many years.

Kim: You are getting too close and I feel too vulnerable. Plus you are too far away and I can't come easily for an emergency appointment if I need one.

Bill: I understand and I think this isn't a good time to end treatment. So let's talk for a minute and see if we can get you through until the next appointment. You can find a way to be vulnerable and protected. And you can modulate the distance and closeness to make it work for you. I can be right there with you while I am here. You can be right here with me while you are there. I can be as far away as you need me to be and as close as you need me to be. And I can be far away and close at the same time.

I went on in a similar vein for a few minutes and then paused.

Kim: Okay, that was helpful. You're right. I can do that. I'll see you next appointment.

I was doing a consultation at a hospital in the West with one of the facility's most challenging borderline patients, Elizabeth. She had been through years of in-patient and out-patient therapy at the hospital and had continually frustrated and ultimately defeated the staff's attempts to help her. She was depressed, suicidal, self-mutilating, and defiant. I told her who I was and that I

knew only a few things about her—that she had been depressed and suicidal for some time.

Bill: How long have you been so depressed? Just a few years or for a long time?

Elizabeth: Since I was eight years old.

Bill: Since you were eight. That's a long time. I am surprised you have lasted this long, being suicidal and depressed.

Elizabeth: Well, two times over the years I almost succeeded in killing myself.

Elizabeth told me that nothing, not medications or therapy, had really helped her depression. I was curious how she had kept herself alive despite the suicidality and the level and duration of depression with which she had to live. She told me that she actually did not want to die. She had struggled against the depression so long because she wanted to live. Nobody really understood that, Elizabeth said, because she was always talking about killing herself.

Bill: You know, I was watching the TV news show, *60 Minutes*, a few weeks ago. Mike Wallace was interviewing this woman [we'll call her Jackie, because I can't remember well enough] who had some sort of degenerative illness and she was fighting through the courts for the right to die.

Wallace asked her: "Why are you suicidal?"

"I am not suicidal," Jackie responded. "I just don't want to live like this and I want the right to choose to die."

Wallace responded, "Well, you are fighting for the right
to die. You say you want to die. You must not want to
live."

"No, I want to live. I just don't want to live like this,"
Jackie said. "I love life."

"Come on," Wallace scoffed. "You are depressed. You
want to die. You are suicidal."

Jackie gave up trying to make him understand her complex
feelings at that point.

By this time I was practically shouting at the screen: Mike, listen to her, for God's sake. She wants to live. She wants to
die. She doesn't want to live like this and she wants the
right to die.

Jackie's story was complicated and inclusive of contradictory
feelings and realities. Could be, I told myself, it's too complex
for network television. Perhaps they could get it on NPR or
PBS.

Bill: [to Elizabeth] I have the
sense that's the way it is with
you; You have lived all this
time because you want to
live. You have fought against
this depression since you
were 8 years old and have
made it this far—by luck, or
because the angels were
watching over you, or because someone cared for you at
times, but most likely because you just kept yourself

going. You want to live and you don't want to live like this.

Elizabeth: That's it exactly. No one has understood that. I'm suicidal and I'm not.

Okay. Enough stories.

(I could go on and on. Ask my wife.)

Are you ready to learn how to be an Inclusive Therapy master? As you might expect, it's incredibly simple and subtly complex.

Here we go.

For every complex question, there is usually a simple answer— and it's usually wrong.

—H.L. Menken

1. Three Basic Methods of Inclusive Therapy

There are just three *basic* methods of Inclusive Therapy:

1. **Give the person permission to and permission not to have to** experience or be something. For example, you can say, "You can feel angry and you don't have to feel angry." Or, "It's okay to be sexual and you don't have to be sexual." Be careful, however, when giving permission about *actions*. We'll get into this in the text, but you don't want to give permission for harmful actions or you may wind up spending a lot of unwanted time with lawyers.

2. **Suggest the possibility of having seeming opposites or contradictions coexist** without conflict. For example, you can say, "You can tell me and not tell me about the abuse." Or, "You can forgive and not forgive at the same time."

3. **Allow for the opposite possibility** when speaking about the way it was, is, or will be. You can say, "You'll either get better or you won't." "That was either a terrible thing or it wasn't." Or, "I'm shy except when I'm not."

From these three basic methods, I draw twenty-six *applied* methods (or techniques.)

I don't want to do Inclusive Therapy a disservice here. I have striven to make Inclusive Therapy as simple and clear as possible, but I fear that at the outset you will see only the simplicity and not recognize the depth and subtlety of this approach.

One could spend many years exploring the implications and variations of these three seemingly simple methods. I also fear that some readers will get only the cheap version of inclusion, thinking they can maneuver people into feeling or getting better by sounding like they are being inclusive. This approach involves deeply understanding and communicating the complex and contradictory character of human experience. You can't fake sincerity for long. People see through it.

These three basic methods are not in any hierarchical or sequential order. And there can be some overlap among them. This is also true of the 26 subsidiary methods (or techniques) that I have found to put the inclusive idea into practice.

Pieces of Inclusive Therapy have been put forth by various theorists and therapies over the years. Freud wrote about how words and feelings often contain or suggest their opposites. Jungian psychology articulated the "shadow" side of the human psyche. Gestalt Therapy concerned itself with integrating unintergated, devalued aspects of self and experience. Dialectical Behavioral Therapy included the dialectical method for use with ambivalent "borderline" clients. In light of this, I am sure that, after this book is published, I will get many letters telling me that some of the pieces of Inclusive Therapy have been part of other approaches. By condensing the main methods of Inclusive Therapy into three categories, I hope to present these various aspects in a manner that makes them accessible and lends them to easy mastery.

Let's proceed to the basic methods and the 26 particular techniques.

The *Permissive* Method

Permission is the first basic method of Inclusive Therapy. Most therapists probably already use this method because many clients come to therapy stuck on the feeling that they shouldn't be feeling, thinking, or acting as they do. Most therapists are good at helping clients accept and feel less ashamed of their experience. Here you will learn a few distinctions and get some clarity on how to use this method better within the context of a therapy premised on inclusion.

1.1   Give permission to

GIVE PERMISSION FOR ANY AND ALL EXPERIENCES, FEELINGS, THOUGHTS, AND FANTASIES THE PERSON MAY HAVE.

Let the client know it is OK to have automatic experiences such as sensations, involuntary thoughts, feelings, and images. Of course, you must always be careful to distinguish these from *plans* and *actions* (not all of which are okay).

A friend of mine, a therapist in Sweden, Klas Grevelius, saw a woman, Eva, for her first session. He couldn't seem to get a fix on why precisely Eva was coming to therapy. She had lots of vague com-  plaints about her life, but nothing con- crete that Klas could find as a *source* of discontent. She was unhappy in her job, in her marriage, and with her social life, but Eva couldn't really say what was wrong or what she wanted to change. Klas suggested that she return for another appointment, but that unless he could find something they could work on, per- haps they couldn't work together. When Eva returned the next week, she was Klas's last appointment of an 11-hour day (during which he had missed his dinner due to an emergency with another client and he had developed a strong headache). The woman started again with her vague complaints and Klas, who is generally very patient and compassionate, began to show his fatigue. He became increasingly frustrated, and his headache grew as he listened to her.

Klas: [finally bursting out] What is it that is really bothering you? Out with it!

Eva: [replying without hesitation] **My horse. It's my horse. He died two years ago and I can't get over it. My husband and friends say it is crazy to grieve so much over a horse, but he was my best friend. I miss him so.**

Klas then said something similar to what I say to my clients.

Klas: Who made the rule that you are supposed to be over your grief in two years? You may grieve this horse for the rest of your life. There is nothing wrong with that. But now I can see what we can do in therapy. I can help support you in standing up to your husband and friends so you can have room to grieve in your own way and time.

Eva was relieved and pulled out pictures of the horse. She cried as she showed them to Klas and recounted some of her memories of the horse. At the end of the session, Klas asked Eva when she wanted to return and she said she didn't need to return. She could handle both her grief as well as answer her husband and friends now that she felt she wasn't crazy or wrong for still grieving for her beloved companion.

The point here is that some people need permission to feel what they feel.

And, as you will see shortly, it is just as important for some people to receive permission not to feel what they don't feel.

 This applied method often involves normalizing or helping people realize that their experience is either fairly common or at least within the range of human experience. We also try to help people distinguish between

feelings, fantasizing, or thinking something and actually doing it or planning to do it. It's okay to feel so angry with someone you want to throttle them. It's *not* okay to throttle them.

Practice: Giving permission to

Okay. I've already got this approach down. I've been doing it for a number of years. It's time for *you* to practice. When I read a book, I must admit, I typically skip the exercises and go right on to the next bit. You certainly can do that. But I didn't put these exercises here just to take up space. I think they can help you get a little experience with these applied methods before you use them with clients. So, I invite you to linger for a moment and practice.

(Of course, it's also okay if you don't do the exercises.)

EXAMPLES **Client: I'm getting really scared as I remember his voice.**
Therapist: It's okay to be scared. Just let yourself feel what you're feeling as much as possible.

Client: Sometimes I daydream about running away and leaving my husband and kids.
Therapist: I've heard other women say that. With them, it's often been a combination of having taken on too much in combination with disappointment with some aspect of marriage and family life. I don't know if that is true for you, but I think it's okay to have those thoughts. *Planning* to leave is a different matter, of course.

In this practice section and those that follow, I give you some client statements and you give a response to each. No need for perfection. You won't be graded. You should, however, try to

respond in a way that exhibits the aspect of Inclusive Therapy
we are exploring. These are designed to get you to engage in
the process.

TRY IT!   **Client: I love my wife, but it's terrible—I keep having these
                 fantasies about this guy at the gym.
                 Therapist:**

                 **Client: I don't know what is wrong with me. I love my baby,
                 but sometimes I have images of him having been thrown
                 against the wall. What is wrong with me?
                 Therapist:**

1.2   Give permission not to have to

GIVE PERMISSION NOT TO HAVE TO EXPERIENCE, FANTASIZE, THINK,
FEEL, OR DO SOMETHING.

Let clients know that they do not have to feel any particular
feeling. Nor do they have to feel compelled by any experience
or be required to initiate any particular action. Sometimes people seem to need permission *not* to have to feel something or
do something.

I once had a client, Michael, who came to therapy because he
was concerned that there was something wrong with him
because he hadn't cried for his father after his father had died
over a year ago. He had been very close to his father, missed
him, and was sad when he had died. Yet Michael had never
cried.

After hearing his story, I told him that grieving was an individual experience and there were no hard and fast rules for it.
Perhaps he would cry when something triggered it sometime
in the future. Perhaps he would never cry. Perhaps he grieved
differently from other people.

He was silent for a time as he considered this.

Michael: It's okay not to cry for my father, then?
Bill: Yeah.

Immediately he began to cry.

Another example is a client of mine, Linda, who was having disturbing fantasies of hurting her baby. Linda felt that sooner or later she would be compelled to act on them. I told her we could practice the skill of having fantasies or images, and *not* acting on them as a way of increasing her confidence in her ability to continue to restrain herself. I suggested that she imagine putting an axe in my skull and throwing me out the window of the second-story office we were in. At first this terrified Linda, but as she did it, in this and further practice sessions, she discovered that it got easier to separate her fantasies from her potential actions.

Another client needed permission not to take care of others' needs before she noticed her own. Yet another person needed permission not to have to be a nice guy all the time (which had often led him to agree to do things he didn't really want to do).

The message here is:

You *don't* have to act on your feelings or fantasies. It's okay to
have them, though. It doesn't necessarily mean anything
bad about you to have them.

Practice: Giving permission not to have to

This technique is used when people feel as if they *have to* feel, do, or be something. Gently let them know this isn't required.

EXAMPLES   Client: I'm getting really scared as I remember his voice.
Therapist: You don't have to be scared. I'm right here and he is not. That is the past. This is the present.

Client: I say "Yes" when I'm thinking "No!"
Therapist: You don't have to say yes. He is making it your problem when it is really his problem.

Client: What if he gets upset?
Therapist: You don't have to take that on. Again, he is making this your problem and it is really his.

Okay. Practice time again.

Remember that this is *practice*. It's okay to make mistakes, be stymied, not have a clue, try and fail.

(You might notice how I am cleverly being congruent by giving you permission *not* to have to do the exercises, to make mistakes, not to know, and so on.)

TRY IT!   Client: I feel I have to take care of everyone.
Therapist:

Client: I can't really remember my abuse. All the books I read say that if I can't remember, I can't heal.
Therapist:

Theory Break: Injunctions

This book is mostly about a practical mode of therapy, but I know some of you like a bit of theory mixed in as roughage with your practical methods. So I'll throw you a bone or two (to mix my metaphors).

One way to think of the presenting problem in therapy is that it reflects an injunction. Injunctions are ideas or beliefs that guide our actions and organize our experience. Sometimes we are not conscious of them. They can be thought of as conclusions that people have made about themselves or ideas that other people have suggested to them or told them are true.

I have found there to be *two* main types of injunctions:

1. **Inhibiting Injunctions** such as can't/shouldn't/don't. These injunctions arise in judgments like: "You shouldn't feel sexual feelings"; "I can't be angry"; "Big boys don't cry"; or "Girls who are sexual are sluts."
2. **Intrusive/Compelling Injunctions** such as have to/should/ must. This form of injunction is expressed in these ways: "You must always be perfect"; "I have to hurt myself"; "I should always smile and be happy"; "Males must be strong and take care of females"; or "Females should take care of others' needs."

The 26 applied methods of Inclusive Therapy are designed to be *counter-injunctions*. They are designed to free people from the inhibitions, compulsions (in the form of feelings or thoughts), or feelings of shame that the injunctions invite. Permission is the most obvious method to help free people from these unhelpful injunctions. This is because permission statements mirror injunctions nicely.

Permission to is designed to help people escape from inhibiting injunctions.

- It's okay to cry if you're male.
- Girls can be sexual and good.
- It's okay to get angry.

Permission not to have to is designed to help people escape from intrusive injunctions.

- You don't have to be perfect.
- You don't have to hurt yourself to deal with your difficult feelings.
- You don't always have to be strong.
- You don't always have to take care of others to the neglect of your own needs.

While giving permission is the most direct way to address injunctions, remember that the other methods can also be helpful with undoing the hold injunctions have on people.

1.3   Give both permissions at once

GIVE PERMISSION TO AND NOT TO HAVE TO.

Give both permissions to cover all the bases. Although you can give either form of permission (permission to or permission not to), I have sometimes found it more useful to give *both* permissions at the same time.

For example:

You can feel angry *and* you don't have to feel angry.
It's okay to be sexual *and* you don't have to be sexual.

If you only give one type of permission, clients might feel pressured to only experience one part of the whole or they might find the other part emerging in a more compelling and disturbing way.

For example, you might say:

It's okay to remember.

The client might then respond by declaring:

But I don't want to remember!

Instead you could have said:

It's okay to remember and you don't have to remember.

If you address your client in this way, he or she won't typically experience a bounce-back response.

Practice: Giving both permissions at once

This technique is helpful when people show ambivalence or when they bounce from one side to another in their feelings or thoughts.

EXAMPLES   **Client: I'm getting really scared as I remember his voice.**
Therapist: It's okay to be scared and you don't have to be scared.

Client: Sometimes I daydream about running away and leaving my husband and kids.
Therapist: It's okay to have those fantasies. And let's see if we can find another way to deal with what is going on in your life, your marriage, or your family so you don't have to have those fantasies.

This time you may have to be more creative in your responses because sometimes it sounds a little weird to say:

It's okay to and you don't have to.

Try to find some way that sounds more natural but gets the same message across.

TRY IT!   **Client: I want to quit my job, but I am afraid if I go out on my own I will fail or won't make enough to pay the bills.**
Therapist:

Client: I am angry all the time.
Therapist:

1.4   Normalize

SPEAK ABOUT THE CONCERN SO AS TO CONVEY THAT IT IS IN THE
REALM OF NORMAL HUMAN EXPERIENCE, RATHER THAN AN EXOTIC
OR TERRIBLE THING.

Another way to give permission is to normalize. This means to
help people realize that their experience—especially aspects of
their experience they think are wrong, bad, shameful, or
weird—are within the range of typical human experiences.
People who come to therapy often feel as if they are the only
ones who have ever felt this way or had this particular problem.

Practice: Normalizing the client's experience

You might tell a story that shows the client's experience to be
common. Or you might commiserate about a similar sense you
have had in relation to what the client is experiencing.

EXAMPLES   **Client: I think about suicide sometimes.**

**Therapist: Actually, I have considered suicide in the past, and
most people I've talked to in my counseling have at one
time or another thought about it. Did you seriously consider doing yourself in or did you made specific plans
recently?**

**Client: We're having a rough time being a blended family. The
kids resent him as my new husband.**

**Therapist: Maybe you expected there to be instant intimacy
or closeness, or you hoped things would gel more
quickly. Most people find they have "lumpy" families for
quite a while before they get blended.**

I often tell stories—about myself, other clients (appropriately disguised), or other people I know or about whom I have read—to help my clients feel as if their experiences are normal or valid. The point is to find way to help clients feel as if their experiences are okay. You might encourage them to read self-help books on the relevant topic or memoirs about others who have similar conditions. You could point them toward support groups for people in their situation.

TRY IT!   **Client: I feel as if everyone is talking behind my back.**
Therapist:

Client: She's oversensitive.
Therapist:

The *Yin-Yang* Method

Inclusion of seeming opposites is the second basic method of Inclusive Therapy. This is the Yin-Yang Method. Opposites go together and, as the ancient symbol shows, each contains a piece of the other. Asian cultures seem to have this concept down better than most Western cultures.

While most of the examples I will give are dualities, this method also lends itself to including pluralities (more than two options). In practice this is often done by several sequences in which dualities are included. For example I might say:

You could want to quit therapy and want to continue. Or you could want to continue but find a way to slow down a bit since you are so overwhelmed. Or you might want to take a break for a time and return when the changes you have made have been consolidated.

The basic idea is that there doesn't need to be a contradiction between seeming opposites so long as we can expand our understanding of experience so as to include them.

1.5 Include opposite or contradictory feelings

INCLUDE, USUALLY WITH AN *AND* IN BETWEEN, SEEMINGLY OPPOSITE OR CONTRADICTORY FEELINGS.

Our language and our culture invite us to identify with or consider only one feeling at a time. The Yin-Yang Method involves recognizing this aspect of Western culture and inviting the client to consider a more complex version of their feeling life.

This more complex outlook will occasionally include seeming contradictions. I say *seeming* because they may not be contradictory at all but merely appear so to the client or others.

Practice: Including opposite or contradictory feelings

As noted above, the aim is to include, usually with an *and* in between, seeming opposites.

EXAMPLES **Client: I really hate my kids.**

Therapist: From what you have told me before, my sense is that you hate them and love them.

Client: I love him but I can't take another beating.

Therapist: You don't want to leave the relationship and you feel you have to leave.

Remember to use the word *and,* not *or* or *but,* when you respond. And remember that sometimes what clients feel to

be opposites may not appear so to you. For example, I had a client for whom feeling close and connected to someone didn't go with feeling sexual, so for her the opposite feelings would be something like:

You can feel connected and sexual.

TRY IT!   **Client: I think about suicide sometimes.**
Therapist:

Client: I want to move to another state and take that new job but I am afraid I'll fail and have to move back in with my parents.
Therapist:

1.6 Include opposite or contradictory aspects of self or others

INCLUDE, AGAIN USUALLY WITH AN *AND* IN BETWEEN, SEEMINGLY OPPOSITE OR CONTRADICTORY *ASPECTS* OF SELF OR OTHERS.

We often identify with or consider only one aspect of ourselves or our experience. We also do this when thinking about other people. This aspect of the Yin-Yang Method involves recognizing, and inviting clients to consider, a more complex version of themselves or others.

I visited Japan some years ago and, during a tour of Tokyo, the guide pointed out a Shinto temple. She told us that perhaps 80% of Japanese people practice the Shinto religion. A few blocks later, she pointed out a Buddhist shrine and said that 70% of Japanese practice Buddhism. A few people recognized a contradiction as they added the percentages. In response to their quizzical expressions, our guide said that, for Japanese people, there is no contradiction or problem in practicing two different religions. In the West, however, this is very illogical. We tend to use a binary kind of logic (either/or). Asian cultures often use an inclusive kind of logic (both/and).

Meredith Brooks, the rock songwriter, captures this complex, but not, finally, contradictory aspect of people.

In "Bitch," Brooks sings:

I'm a bitch, I'm a lover, I'm a child, I'm a mother, I'm a sinner, I'm a saint.

In an interview with her that I read, Brooks shed some light on this song by explaining that she kept having relationships break up because she was so changeable and contradictory. Finally, Brooks said that she realized that she was just that way—she was all of those things about which she sang. Her way to address this was to stop trying to be "good" at the beginning of relationships because she knew eventually the truth would leak out.

Practice: Including opposite or contradictory aspects of self or others

You are not trying to persuade clients to be more inclusive with this applied method. You are asking them to recognize and articulate the opposites that already exist within their lives, their character, and their experience.

EXAMPLES **Client: I am really lazy.**

Therapist: Yet, last weekend, you helped your best friend move on your two days off. So it seems that you are lazy and not lazy.

Client: She can be so cold one minute and then so loving another.

Therapist: She's cold and loving.

Remember to use the word *and,* not *or* or *but,* when you respond.

These seeming opposites are not necessarily opposites in the dictionary. We are not just concerned with antonyms. They are opposites in the client's experience. For example, a client might experience sexuality and being good as opposites. Or he might experience being vulnerable and being male as opposites.

I once heard a poet giving a lecture in which he said:

> The opposite of exhaustion is not necessarily rest. It is wholeheartedness.

This kind of creative thinking is useful in imagining what the opposites are for clients.

TRY IT!   **Client: I can't let her know I am scared she might die. I have to be strong for her.**
Therapist:

Client: I feel so dirty when I ask for what I want sexually.
Therapist:

1.7   Use tag questions

INCLUDE ANOTHER SIDE OF THE EQUATION IN A SINGLE SENTENCE.

This involves including an opposite at the end of the sentence, in the form of a question. When I studied with Milton Erickson, he once told me:

If you don't say the *no*, the patient has to say it.

He often bypassed this "resistance" and negativity by including the opposite in the form of a tag question or statement. The French do this when they end their statements with the phrase, *n'est pas,* which roughly translates to *is it not so?*

Erickson would say to a client, in the course of therapy:

You really want to change, *don't you?*

Or:

You are really having trouble with making that change, *are you not?*

If he were doing hypnosis with the client, Erickson might say something like:

You are sure you are still awake, *are you not?*

Or:

You're not in trance, *are you?*

Practice: Using tag questions

Include a question at the end of a reflective statement you make to the client. This question, the tag question, should contain some opposite to the statement.

EXAMPLES   **Client: I really hate my kids.**
Therapist: You really hate them, don't you?

Client: I can't stay in that job a day longer.
Therapist: You can't, can you?

Use phrases like:

* ..., are you not?
* ..., do you not?
* ..., do you?
* ..., can you?

Place these phrases at the end of your sentences. This is designed to recognize the sometimes unspoken aspects of a client's experience.

TRY IT!   **Client: I don't know if I can change.**
Therapist:

Client: I want to move, to another state and take that new job but I am afraid I'll fail and have to move back in with my parents.
Therapist:

Theory Break: The Importance of *And*

Years ago, when it was in vogue, I had a bit of training in Gestalt Therapy. One of the ideas Gestalt was touting was the use of the word *and* instead of *but*.

The sentence:

I want to stay in bed, but I have to go to work.

was turned into:

I want to stay in bed *and* I have to go to work.

This notion came from the Gestalt idea of honoring and including all aspects of people's experience as valid and not necessarily in conflict. Most of the rest of what I learned in those days seems to have slipped away, but that piece stayed. I like the idea of using the word *and* to connect things that are usually not connected and thereby to dissipate potential conflicts.

Reflecting with the word *and* as a conjunction can help clients who may be acting out of only one side of their experience. We can often help them recognize and validate the other side (or both sides).

Consider these examples:

You want to live *and* you don't want to continue living in this kind of pain.
You want to stay married *and* you want out.
You feel angry enough to hit her *and* it's not okay to hit her.

1.8 Use oxymoron and apposition of opposites

INCLUDE THE OTHER SIDE OF THE EQUATION IN A PHRASE CONSIST-
ING OF OPPOSITES (OXYMORON) OR IN SEPARATE PARTS OF THE SAME
PHRASE OR SENTENCE.

Erickson had two other similar ways to include opposites. He
would use oxymoron (this word itself comes from combining

two ancient Greek words mean-
ing *sharp* and *dull*) or put these
opposites further apart but still in
the same phrase or sentence
(apposition of opposites).

One time Erickson was treating a
young woman who had been
compulsively sexual. She told

Erickson she had been sexually abused by her father and ever
since then had felt compelled to have sex with any man she
met even while being terrified of a man's penis. Penises seemed
threatening to her. Because she was unwilling or unable to stop
acting out sexually, one of Erickson's first suggestions was that
she begin to take a "vicious pleasure" in reducing those hard,
threatening penises to limp, dangling, helpless things. Vicious
pleasure is a wonderful oxymoron, isn't it?*

Another time Erickson reported that a woman came into his
office and sat down in an "elaborately casual" manner. Another
wonderful oxymoron.

---

* See this and other relevant case examples in O'Hanlon and Angela Hexum (eds.) (1990). *An
Uncommon Casebook* (New York: Norton).

Here is a list of some of my favorite oxymoronic phrases so you can get the sense of them.

- Awfully nice
- Exact estimate
- Found missing
- Same difference
- Almost exactly
- Sweet sorrow
- Now, then . . .
- Working vacation
- Terribly pleased
- Tight slacks
- Definite maybe
- Pretty ugly.

Other times Erickson would spread the opposites farther apart. He might say that you could be engaged in detaching from some person who was bad for you. This is like an oxymoron (*engaged detachment*) but the tension is extended through the entire sentence because the relationship is not between verb and adverb or noun and adjective. We refer to this as the apposition of opposites.

You might remember to remember this or you might remember to forget it if you don't need to remember it.

(This is getting confusing, isn't it? Oh, forget it.)

This is a good example of apposition: Some people change by staying the same and other stay the same by changing. Or the more things change, the more they stay the same. (*Plus ça change, plus c'est la meme chose*, as the French say; these French are very inclusive, *n'est pas?*)

Practice: Using oxymoron and apposition of opposite

Pick two opposite concepts and include them in a single phrase or sentence. Make them clinically relevant to the client.

EXAMPLES   **Client: I am anxious about the upcoming exam.**
Therapist: You can calmly observe that anxiety to notice whether it helps you or not.

Client: I can't stay in that job a day longer.
Therapist: You can be impatiently patient until the right time comes to leave and leave not a day too soon or too late.

Remember the Yin-Yang symbol and imagine that each feeling or aspect of a client or his or her situation needs to be included. Think of a creative phrase that captures both aspects of the opposites. Put that phrase into a sentence or a question. Oxymoron is condensed into a single adjectival or adverbial phrase. Apposition of opposites is spread out through the sentence.

TRY IT!   **Client: I don't know if I can change.**
Therapist:

Client: I think I'm afraid of succeeding and afraid of failing.
Therapist:

1.9   Validate the "resistance"

JOIN WITH, VALUE, ACCEPT, AND INCLUDE ANY "RESISTANCE" THE
CLIENT SHOWS OR EXPRESSES.

I put the word *resistance* in quotation marks because I think a
lot of what is seen as resistance is really a reflection of misun-
derstanding and inflexibility on
the part of the therapist. I also
hold that much of what therapists call *resistance* reflects
legitimate concerns on the
part of clients. We should take
their "resistance" seriously

and validate it. In addition, in the context of Inclusive Therapy,
valuing and accepting the resistance is a way to defuse the
power the resistance has to block desired change.

Practice: Validating the "resistance"

This can't be faked sincerity. The inclusive therapist really sees
the expressed concern, what seems to be resistance, as valid
and legitimate. The therapist does his or her best to include
those concerns and take those concerns seriously.

EXAMPLES   Client: I just can't do that homework you gave me.

Therapist: All right. It may be that I suggested something
that isn't right for you. Or maybe there is something we
haven't talked about or dealt with yet that we need to
address before you do this. Or it could be something else
altogether. Do you have any sense of it?

Client: I don't want to work on the marriage. I'm done. After she had the affair, love died for me.

Therapist: Okay. You came to therapy with her. What do you think we can do here that might be helpful if it doesn't involve working on the marriage?

This applied method or technique involves trying to understand the resistance. If you can't understand the resistance, then you are to try to accept the legitimacy of clients' concerns and struggles. Be careful not to patronize.

TRY IT!   Client: Nothing works. I've tried everything.
Therapist:

Client: I really can't afford your fees, but I don't feel that anyone else can help me.
Therapist:

1.10   Contain the "resistance" or the problem

ACCEPT AND ALLOW THE RESISTANCE OR THE PROBLEM, BUT
CONTAIN IT IN SPACE, TIME, OR MODE OF EXPRESSION.

This is another one I got from Erickson. He would sometimes
be in the process hypnotizing one of his patients and the
patient would be having difficulty going into trance. Erickson
would then remark:

**You seem to be having a great deal of difficulty going into
trance in that chair. I suggest you move to the other
chair, and we'll continue.**

He reported that this would often result in the patient leaving
his or her resistance in the first chair. Or Erickson, on finding
that his patient was unwilling to talk about certain painful or
shameful experiences, would
suggest that the patient tell him
about everything but the particular years during which the difficult experiences occurred.

In a similar fashion, Erickson
would suggest that clients continue to have their symptoms or
problems while encouraging them to limit these symptoms or
problems to fifteen minutes per night. During that period they
should intensely experience the symptoms or perform the
problems. This had the effect of containing the unwanted experiences in time.

Another way Erickson would do this was to suggest that clients express their resistance or problem in a different, often more useful, way. A man who was hospitalized psychiatrically after losing his business and going bankrupt spent his days crying and moving his hands back and forth in front of him as if pushing something away from himself. Erickson read his history in the man's medical chart, walked up to him, and said;

You seem like a man who has had his ups and downs in life.

Erickson proceeded to move the man's hands in an up–and–down manner until the man began to take up the new movement pattern. Some days later, when he observed the man was still following the new pattern, Erickson took the man down to the occupational therapy department. There he strapped some sandpaper on both of the patient's hands and placed the man's hands around an old, painted table leg that was being refinished. At first the man's hands just randomly touched the table leg but, after a short time, the man began deliberately sanding the table leg. He went on to refinish the table, then he began fashioning chess sets. The patient  got rather good at making these chess sets and soon was selling them to staff and other patients. He was released from the hospital soon thereafter.*

---

* For descriptions of these strategies and cases see Jay Haley (1985). *Conversations with Milton H. Erickson, M.D.* (Washington, DC: Triangle Press).

Practice: Containing the "resistance" or the problem

Think of a way to allow or encourage the person to have the problem but in some more contained or useful way.

This approach requires some creativity as well as an attitude of acceptance so as to work with sources of resistance and problems rather than opposing them.

EXAMPLES **Client: I can't stop picking at my scabs. I am at myself for hours each night, picking myself bloody.**
Therapist: How about this? Try giving yourself permission to pick them for 5 minutes each hour from 6 p.m. to 9 p.m. That would both be giving you some compulsion and some control.

Client: I criticize myself for the slightest mistake.
Therapist: All right. I'd like you to choose one thing you think you did wrong and write about it for the next week. Exhaust the subject. Go into every absurd detail about what you did wrong and what it says about you.

Sometimes this technique is seen as a form of paradox, but I think of it differently. Paradox involves getting the client to deliberately exaggerate the problem or implies encouraging the resistance. Containing the resistance or problem is a bit different. It involves scheduling, localizing, or otherwise containing the expression of the problem or resistance. The problem or resist-

ance is accepted, but now in a more limited and less destructive sphere.

TRY IT! **Client:** I surf the Internet for porn every night and I have spent $900 in the past month calling sex lines. I've tried to stop, but have failed. I need help.
Therapist:

Client: I obsess about my ex-husband. I can't seem to let go, even though I'm now in a good relationship.
Therapist:

The *Or Not* Method

Allowing or including other possibilities (exceptions) is the third basic method of Inclusive Therapy. This method recognizes that there is often an unspoken complexity to life and to clients' situations. This method can remind us and our clients that there may be another side (at least) to the story.

1.11   Include or allow for the opposite possibility

ARTICULATE THE UNSPOKEN OPPOSITE POSSIBILITY.

When clients make predictions or definitive pronouncements about things they cannot know for certain, I often find a way to include the opposite possibility without being sarcastic or invalidating. I do the same when I find myself making similar predictions or pronouncements.

Those of you who know about solution-based (i.e., solution-oriented or solution-focused) therapies know many techniques and methods for identifying exceptions to the rule of the problem. One usually asks about times when clients would have expected the problem to happen and it didn't.

Consider these examples:

Can you recall a time when you thought you would binge, but instead you resisted the urge?

Can you tell me about a time when John was able to sit quietly and surprised you or himself?

Practice: Including or allowing for the opposite possibility

Think about unspoken possibilities or opposites.

Physicist Neils Bohr proclaimed:

> A great truth is a truth whose opposite is also a great truth.

Whenever the client suggests a single-minded truth, remind yourself and the client, if appropriate, that there is another possibility. Remember that there are usually at least two sides to every story. Include, ever so gently and respectfully, the opposite possibility when generalized pronouncements or predictions are made. In this way, these generalizations won't become a booby trap for either therapist or client.

EXAMPLES   **Client: I'm never going to drink again. This time, unlike all the others, I've got it licked.**

Therapist: Time will tell. You'll either stop this time or not. You've gone back to it before, but everyone who has stopped for good has stopped one time or another. This could be your time.

Client: I'm never going to fall in love again. Relationships are too hard.

Therapist: You may not fall in love again, but if you do, let's make sure you make better choices.

This is not just an applied method for getting to the positives or the solutions when the client discusses problems. It is also a way for identifying false and unrealistic positives. Both clients and therapists can get into these unrealistic positives. I once saw a cartoon about a therapy session.

Client: I think I see the light at the end of the tunnel.

Therapist: How do you know that's not another train coming?

Allowing for the opposite possibility can temper the unthinking and naive enthusiasm in which both therapists and clients sometimes become wrapped. Naive enthusiasm may leave us unprepared for setbacks or bad news.

TRY IT! **Client: I'm going to get the job. I'm sure of it.**
Therapist:

Client: Everyone is stupid. No one cares about anyone else.
Therapist:

Theory Break: The Limits of Our Knowledge

I remember reading a story about a physician in Australia who became convinced that ulcers were caused by bacteria (*H. pylori*). Up to that time, physicians and the general public held the view that ulcers were caused by stress and anxiety. When this physician—not a researcher, just a general physician—began to write and talk about this new idea in medical settings, he was pilloried and dismissed. He finally resorted to ingesting some *H. pylori* himself, which soon resulted in ulcers. It still took many years, but, finally, others were persuaded of the truth of his idea. Subsequent experimentation and testing of samples from ulcer patients confirmed the hypothesis. Now the general view is that ulcers are caused by bacteria.

What's the point?

If you were asserting some years ago that ulcers were caused by stress, you could have hedged your bets and been closer to the truth if you had said: Ulcers are caused by stress (or they aren't entirely). Our knowledge proceeds by fits and starts. Each time we assert that we know the truth, we may have only part of the truth or but a distorted truth. What I would say if I were speaking about it now is: Ulcers are caused by bacteria (although there may be other factors and we may not yet fully understand the role bacteria plays). Because someday we may find that while *H. pylori* bacteria are present in all cases of ulcers, there may be another, underlying factor that contributes to their causation.

What does this have to do with psychotherapy? Therapists are continually making assertions of the truth—e.g., pathology is caused by neurological dysfunction; pathology is caused by distorted thinking; pathology is caused by messed up social or familial relationships. These may all be true. Or not (at least not completely).

In the same way, our clients make claims to the truth when they tell us about their problems:

I'll never get over the abuse I suffered. [*Our response could be to silently think, Or you will.*]
This marriage is over. I don't love her any more. [*Or you do love her. Or the marriage is not over.*]

You get the point, I suspect. We don't know for certain what is true. And we certainly don't know what will be true in the future.

I once had a client, Jim, who told me his psychiatrist had informed him that he would have to be on a particular medication for the rest of his life. Jim was feeling very depressed at the information because the medication had some very unpleasant side effects. I responded by telling Jim that only God knew what was going to happen in the future and that, although some psychiatrists confuse themselves with God, they certainly did not have the same power to know the future. Jim laughed and we explored what he could do to cope with the side effects while he was on the medication.

Again it may sound like a paradox, but we can be certain we are uncertain. We must proceed in life as if we are certain of reality and truth but I am suggesting that there be a little *or not* in the back of the mind that reminds us that current conception of truth or reality may be subject to revision as we learn more.

1.12   Employ paradoxical striving

ENCOURAGE PEOPLE TO MAKE THEIR SYMPTOM OR PROBLEM WORSE.

This technique was popularized by Viktor Frankl, the Viennese psychiatrist and founder of Logotherapy. Its origin is associated with a story that once circulated in Austria about a high school that was putting on a play in which one of the parts called for the actor to stutter. Because the students knew one of their classmates stuttered, they asked him if he would like the part. It turned out that he had always harbored a desire to act, but was certain that his speech problem would preclude this possibility. Given the chance, he agreed to play the role. However, when it came time to conduct dress rehearsals, he found that he could not stutter when he deliberately tried to. Frankl heard this story and suggested a similar striving for his patients who stuttered. When some of them found that this method worked for stuttering, Frankl began trying it with other problems. He discovered that, particularly with problems that involved anxiety, paradoxical staring was often effective. (Except when it wasn't, of course.) He used it successfully with problems of impotence (try not to get aroused or have an erection), insomnia (try to stay awake), and panic attacks or phobias (try to make yourself more afraid).

I once consulted on a case in which Nina, a nineteen-year-old woman, was mostly housebound because she feared she would

wet her pants if she was out and couldn't quickly get to a toilet. She knew the fear was irrational, but still it limited her greatly. As she and her therapists sat side by side (on my *cloth* couch, I might add), I asked Nina what the most surprising incident had been in regard to her problem. Her account illustrates the effectiveness of paradoxical striving.

Nina's mother and father were divorced. Of her parents, her mother, Jerry, was more sympathetic about Nina's fears. She could ride in the car with her mother because Jerry had agreed to stop at a moment's notice, only taking a route that Nina had mapped out and on which Nina was aware of the location of every bathroom along the way. Jerry had not come out well financially in the divorce, so she and her daughter were also bound by a common resentment of the father, who had much more money than they did.

One day, Nina's father convinced her to take a short trip with him in his new car. She agreed, but only after her father agreed to stop any time Nina requested. Once Nina got in the car, however, he took off onto the highway and wouldn't stop. As he drove, Nina's father told her that her fears were ridiculous and he wasn't going to indulge her "craziness" like her mother had. Nina began to panic, and she yelled and pleaded with him to stop before she peed in her pants. Her father said: "I'll pay you $500 if you can pee in your pants right now."

Nina was really "pissed" at her father, and she would have liked to pee on the upholstery of that new car of his and get some of his money. But she discovered that, when she deliberately tried, the urge to urinate entirely went away.

Practice: Employing paradoxical striving

Determine what symptoms or issues are getting worse or staying the same when clients try to change them, then encourage them to reverse the direction of their striving. This usually involves getting people to stop trying to change or even getting them to try to make the problem worse.

EXAMPLES **Client: I'm afraid I will faint if I try to call this girl and ask her for a date.**

Therapist: Okay, so how about trying to get yourself terrified before the phone call and see if you can faint and get it out of the way before you make the call. Choose a nice soft place to land, think about calling her, then get yourself into the panic mode and faint.

Client: As soon as I start to enter her vagina, I lose my erection.

Therapist: All right. I'd like you to try an experiment. I'd like to have you try to stop yourself from getting aroused when you two start to mess around sexually. Try to keep your penis flaccid for as long as you can.

A *caution* with this applied method.

Do not suggest that people do harmful, illegal, or destructive acts. This intervention is mainly about including and accepting thoughts or feelings, *not actions*. So you wouldn't suggest that a person attempt suicide more often or get better at cutting themselves. I would recommend caution even using it with the thoughts and feelings involving these kinds of issues.

TRY IT! **Client: I wake up in the middle of the night and can't stop my mind from going round and round. I lose sleep and am exhausted in the morning.**
Therapist:

Client: I obsess about my ex-husband. I can't seem to let go, even though I'm now in a good relationship.
Therapist:

The test of a first-rate intelligence is the ability to hold two opposed ideas in the mind at the same time, and still retain the ability to function.
—F. Scott Fitzgerald

2. Validation and Change

One of the challenges of therapy is balancing the processes of validating and accepting where clients are and yet challenging them to change.

Carl Rogers made the point, in *Client-Centered Therapy,* that accepting people as they are, with unconditional positive regard, can have therapeutic effects. At the same time, those of us who do therapy are all too aware that in many cases such acceptance is not sufficient to bring about change.

On the one hand, if people don't feel they have been heard or validated in what they are presently feeling or in their current point of view, they will often resist change. They will stay locked in a defensive mode. On the other hand, if all we offer is acceptance and warm understanding, people will often settle into a comfortable passivity. Whether the thera-pist challenges or accepts the client, the result can be the same—stagnation.

So, this chapter is about balancing acceptance and challenge, validation and change, acknowledgment and possibility. The applied methods, or techniques, proposed are really just variations on the three basic methods outlined in Chapter 1.

In an almost Zen-like, paradoxical way, I suggest that therapists must accept people where they are and give up wanting clients to change. At the same time, we must invite them to change and challenge them to reach for new possibilities.

Again, language almost deserts us when trying to relate the complexity and subtlety of this idea. I sometimes call these methods *Carl Rogers with a Twist*, because they seem to me to combine the best of what Rogers's client-centered approach has to offer with the possibilities of later developments that seem more directive.

I have heard a saying:

> You've got to be where you are to get where you are going.

This captures the essence of this chapter.

So here are 5 techniques of validation and change.

2.1   Acknowledge with the past tense

LET PEOPLE KNOW YOU HAVE HEARD OR ACCEPTED THEIR FEELINGS, PROBLEMS, OR POINTS OF VIEW, WHILE LOCATING THEM IN THE PAST.

When people come to therapy, they are often so beleaguered or stuck that they don't notice change. They may have become so discouraged that they don't expect change to occur. One of the ways we can invite them to be more available to making or noticing change is to subtly move the problem, feeling, or point of view into the past. This often opens space for present and future possibilities. It can show clients that things have changed or can change.

Practice: Acknowledging with the past tense

Reflect your understanding of what the client has just told you while using the past tense to imply that the issue or problem is in the past and that the present and future offer other possibilities.

EXAMPLES   Client: Whenever I get flashbacks I feel compelled to cut myself.

Therapist: You've felt compelled to cut yourself when you've had flashbacks.

Client: He never does what we tell him to.

Therapist: So he hasn't done what you have asked him to.

Typically, when employing this technique, I focus on the things clients say that seem blaming or discouraging. For example, a person might say:

I am sad.

I don't necessarily respond:

You've been sad.

I'm more likely to use this technique when the person says something like:

Counseling is never going to work for him. He's too rigid.

To that I might respond:

He's seemed to you too rigid to make changes.

I usually target this intervention at statements of impossibility or blame.

I have kept many of the client examples the same in this chapter, because I think it is interesting to learn how many different responses one could give to the same statement. I also hope that *your* different responses will help you distinguish between these methods.

TRY IT!   **Client: I can't assert myself. I get too nervous.**
Therapist:

Client: I get numb from the waist down when I start to have sex.

Therapist:

2.2   Acknowledge with partial instead of global reflections

CHANGE PEOPLE'S STATEMENTS FROM GLOBAL, ALL-OR-NOTHING STATEMENTS INTO MORE MODULATED, PARTIAL STATEMENTS THROUGH REFLECTION.

When people are experiencing specific problems, they often globalize them.

- *Everything* is going wrong.
- *Nobody* understands me.
- *Nothing* works.
- I can *never* keep my mouth shut.

Even if their phrases aren't obviously global, the concept behind them is. They say:

- I *have* to cut myself.
- I *am* depressed.

What is implied, though, is:

- I *always* have to cut myself.
- I am *always* depressed.

Unlike some more educationally-based approaches, I do not try to teach my clients not to generalize or to reflect upon their distorted thinking. I do not explain the concepts of *globalized* and *distorted thinking*. Nor do I encourage clients to ferret out and change their self-talk between sessions. I merely reflect what they have just told me and modify it a little, making it less global and general, but hopefully still keeping it congruent with their felt experience.

As a matter of fact, they will usually respond more adamantly and globally if my reflection is perceived as minimizing or too positive. If I said:

So occasionally you are depressed.

A client might say:

Not occasionally, always!

I usually introduce only small modifications, going from all-or-nothing to *usually, mostly, often, most of the time, almost always, typically,* and so on. Most clients don't even notice the change in wording, but this slight change seems to open them up to new possibilities and allows them to notice exceptions to their generalizations.

Practice: Acknowledging with partial instead of global reflections

Slightly alter people's global statements when reflecting by using modified, incrementally less global words and phrases.

EXAMPLES   Client: I never get a break.
             Therapist: Most of the time things haven't gone your way. It's been hard to get a break.

             Client: He never does what we tell him to.
             Therapist: He hasn't done most of the things you have asked him to.

The words used here are usually modulations in time and number. Here's a list of some of the words and phrases that reflect this method:

- Usually
- Often
- Mainly
- Many
- Typically
- Almost
- Recently
- Most
- Pretty
- Rarely
- Few
- Lately.

TRY IT!   **Client: I can't assert myself. I get too nervous.**
Therapist:

Client: I get numb from the waist down when I start to have sex.
Therapist:

2.3   Acknowledge by changing reality or truth statements into perceptions

REFLECT PEOPLE'S CLAIMS OF TRUTH OR REALITY AS MORE INDIVID-
UAL PERCEPTIONS AND SENSES OF REALITY AND TRUTH.

When people are having problems they often get their individual sense of truth or reality (truth with a little *t*, reality with a
little *r*) confused with Truth or Reality. "I
can't get a job" is not a statement of
the Truth. "I will never get over
this" is not Reality. Of course, to
the person who is experiencing
problems, these statements appear
to be true and to reflect reality. But
that is part of our task as change-agents: helping
people realize that those seemingly unchangeable things are
changeable.

In service of this goal, I reflect what they have just told me as a
statement of their sense of things at this moment, not as an
eternal and unchangeable truth.

Practice: Acknowledging by changing reality or truth statements into perceptions

Remember that you are not trying to manipulate people or
force them to accept your more optimistic appraisal of the situation. You are merely (and subtly) suggesting that their perceptions may not take into consideration all the possibilities.
You do this by reminding them in your reflections that this is
the way they are seeing things or feeling at this moment.

EXAMPLES   Client: I never get a break.

Therapist: It really seems to you like the deck is stacked against you.

Client: He never does what we tell him to.
Therapist: You haven't seen him cooperate much lately.

Note that this last reflection incorporated all three of the applied methods we have covered so far. As long as it doesn't invalidate or disrespect people, or minimize their suffering, feel free to combine these approaches.

Here's another list of some of phrases that reflect this technique:

- Your sense ...
- You can't remember ...
- You've gotten the idea ...
- In your view ...
- As far as you can tell ...
- It seems to you ...
- You haven't really seen ...
- From what you have seen ...
- From what you have experienced ...
- From your perspective ...
- You're pretty convinced ...

TRY IT!   Client: I can't assert myself. I get too nervous.
Therapist:

Client: I get numb from the waist down when I start to have sex.
Therapist:

Theory Break: The 3-D Model and The Inclusive Self

When I was in graduate school, I studied the theories of Jean Piaget. He had a developmental theory that indicated how we humans create a sense of reality and self by means of a relatively predictable series of steps.

At first, Piaget held, infants do not distinguish between themselves and the world, including other people. (It's as if infants are natural Buddhists, experiencing themselves and the world as unified.) As the process of socialization goes on, we start to distinguish ourselves from our environment and from

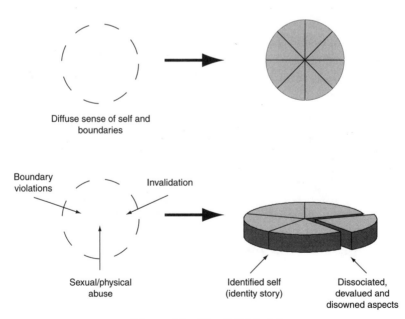

Diffuse sense of self and boundaries

Boundary violations   Invalidation

Sexual/physical abuse   Identified self (identity story)   Dissociated, devalued and disowned aspects

Figure 2.1   The 3-D Model

other people. We gradually construct a sense of identity from our raw experience. And, for the most part, we include much of our raw experience in the identity story we construct.

Like other stories, this identity story doesn't include everything that could be included. Some aspects of experience get left out because they don't fit the main story. Some get left out because we are ashamed of those aspects or have dissociated them in reaction to some trauma. I call this process the *3-D model*, referring to the idea that we tend to Dissociate, Disown, and Devalue.

We either detach (dissociate), not claim as part of our identity (disown), and/or devalue (decide at some level that the aspect is bad, invalid, or worthless) aspects of ourselves or our experience. We identify with only some aspects of ourselves and disidentify with the reminder.

For example, one might grow up in a family in which a child has died. The forbidden topic then might be death and sadness. The devalued feeling or memory of the death would become the dissociated aspect of self.

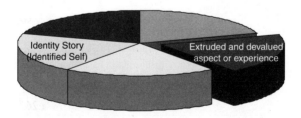

**Figure 2.2   The 3-D Model: Dissociated, Disowned, and
Dissociated Aspects of Experience**

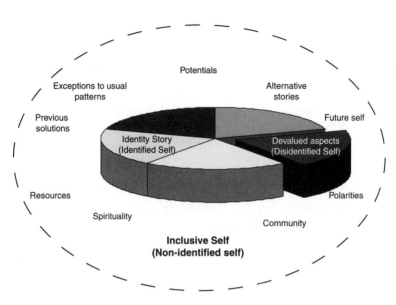

Figure 2.3   The Inclusive Self

Or one might grow up in a family in which sexuality was considered bad or shameful. Then sex might be the devalued, dissociated, and disowned aspect of self that becomes extruded and detached from the identity story.

Mind you, these pieces of experience or self never really go away. They just become detached and are not integrated with the identity story.

So we start out as a 360 degree self and end up as perhaps a 267 degree self. But always, surrounding the story, is the original raw material of experience, including potentials we have not yet developed. I call this the *inclusive self*.

At first, infants don't have the names or experiences to distinguish aspect of themselves like their feelings, their sensations, their memories, their thoughts, and their separate sense of self. We help them, by means of language and cultural concepts, to make these distinctions and therefore to construct their identities from the raw material of undifferentiated experience. We also help them construct a sense of individual identity, an integrated sense of themselves. These *are my feelings, my thoughts, my memories,* and so on.

With most of us, though, we feel ashamed or embarrassed about some aspects of ourselves. If you are a Catholic priest, perhaps you have decided that any sexual thoughts or feelings you have are unacceptable, as they may tempt you to break your vow of chastity, or because you view them as coming from Satan, or because they contain some inappropriate imagery. This leads to the splitting of these thoughts, images or feelings from the identity:

These feelings are not me. I am not like this. I must pray more to get rid of these feelings or images.

This becomes almost an anti-self. It (and this is an interesting word, *it*, because it denotes the *not me*) must be suppressed, hidden or destroyed somehow. It is bad or unacceptable.

The non-identified self contains the larger self, the aspect of oneself that can contain and allow the seeming contradictions complex realities within our experience:

I am giving and selfish. I am frightened and calm.

This non-identified self also contains information that is not well represented in the identity story. Information, for example, regarding times when a person who is usually anxious is able to be calm. Or times when a depressed person laughs and feels more energy.

We will return to this "bigger self" when we visit the topic of spirituality in Chapter 3.

The inclusive self, then, is the well we draw from when we use Inclusive Therapy. We are drawing on the aspects of self that haven't been included in the identity story. The inclusive self contains:

- exceptions to the problem
- connections to alternate stories about oneself and the future
- polarities, resources, and potentials
- the *shadow* self.

The shadow self is the anti-self—the aspects that seem the most unlike us but still show up at times in our experience. Songwriter Billy Joel calls this aspect "The Stranger" in his song of the same name. The Stranger shows up at the most inopportune moments and is the part of ourselves we hide away from ourselves or others. When the shadow or inner stranger has become particularly detached and devalued, it often shows up in an intrusive way, which we'll get to in a moment.

In Inclusive Therapy, we are trying to bring in, value, and include more of the person's experience than they have been including or connecting with so far.

If persons have dissociated, disowned, or detached from aspects of themselves or their experience, they often experience one of two kinds of problems:

- **Inhibition problems,** in which they feel numb, deadened, or dimin-
  ished in some way; or
- **Intrusion problems,** in which they feel dominated by, intruded upon,
  or compelled by certain feelings, images, or impulses.

It's as if a bunch of roommates living together decide that one of their
number is unacceptable and must go. One night the majority conspires to
grab him and throw him out the door. The extruded roommate tries to
get back in the house, but the rest won't let him in. He pounds on the
door and demands to be let in, but they ignore him. After a time, he
seems to give up trying and slumps against the door. This slumped figure
is the inhibition side. The rejected roommate seems to be gone. But after
a time, he decides he's going to get back in the house by hook or by
crook, so he breaks a window and climbs in. The inhibited becomes the
intrusive.

To make this more clear for those in therapy-land, consider someone
who might not remember much about their childhood. All of a sudden,
this person begins to get intrusive flashbacks. Or reflect on the case of
one of my clients, Sandy. Sandy was unable to experience or express
anger. She was just inhibited in that area. That was until, one day, one
of her children was fighting with another of her children and yelled for
her help. Sandy came into the room and began yelling at the kids. They
were shocked: She never got angry. This time, though, Sandy became so
enraged that she threw a lamp across the room. Inhibition was followed
by intrusion.

Inclusive Therapy is designed to deal with these problems by bringing back the missing roommate—by inviting, giving permission for and including whatever the person has dissociated, devalued, or disowned in their experience.

2.4   Reflecting problems as preferences

REPEAT BACK TO THE PERSON WHAT THEY HAVE JUST EXPRESSED AS A
FUTURE PREDILECTION RATHER THAN AS A PAST COMPLAINT.

Problems are usually part of the past. One of our tasks as therapists, while expressing empathy and
understanding for clients and their
problems, is to invite them into
the future. The problem has
occurred. In the future, things
can be different.

This technique works by reflection. It subtly shifts the emphasis
from the past to the future, from what
people do not like to what they would like. Someone might say:

He never listens to me.

I might respond:

So you would like him to listen to you more.

When a client says:

I am so anxious; I cannot go outside.

I might reflect:

**Then you've come here to be able to feel more calm and to
be able to go outside more easily and often.**

These reflections contain several elements:

1. They shift the emphasis from the past to the future.
2. They shift the emphasis from what clients do not want to what they would like.
3. They often refer to what would be gained instead of what would be lost (e.g., "You would like to be more calm," rather than "You'd like to be less anxious.")
4. They often refer to small increments of change rather than big changes (i.e., "You'd like to be a bit more comfortable," rather than, "You like to be totally rid of your anxiety."

Practice: Reflecting problems as preferences

Restate what people have told you as a desire or goal for the future rather than a problem in the past.

EXAMPLES   **Client: I never get a break.**
Therapist: You'd really like to have a few things go your way.

Client: He never does what we tell him to.
Therapist: You like to see him do a few of the things you have asked him to do.

You might need a bit of practice to change statements into the *presence of* something rather than the *absence of* something. And don't worry if you can't find a way to do that. The main thing is to invite clients to switch from the past (and what they don't want), into the future (and what they do want), while validating their experience.

TRY IT!   Client: I can't assert myself. I get too nervous.

Therapist:

Client: I get numb from the waist down when I start to have

sex.

Therapist:

2.5 Acknowledge while adding expectancy or possibilities for change

REFLECTING WHILE ADDING WORDS OR PHRASES THAT GIVE A SENSE THAT CHANGE IS POSSIBLE OR EXPECTED IN THE FUTURE

I once witnessed Milton Erickson do an entire hypnotic induction using expectancy talk. He said:

I don't want you to go into trance too quickly tonight. Before you go into trance, I will want to talk with you about what your unconscious mind will be changing while you are in trance. . . . Not that quickly. . . . That's right, taking your time to go more deeply.

That was about it. He never directly suggested the subject go into trance; it was all done by implication.

This applied method draws on a similar sensibility. People are influenced by expectancy and implication. The therapist adds this sense of expectation to the standard reflections offered as validation.

Practice: Acknowledging while adding expectancy or possibilities for change

In order to master this technique it might help you to imagine the person having already accomplished the change for which you want to communicate an expectation.

For example, if a client says he cannot ask a girl out for a date, you might imagine him already having done it and reflect:

When you ask a girl out, you'll feel as if you have really accomplished something and been brave.

Because you have already visualized it happening, you can speak from the expectancy that it will happen.

EXAMPLES **Client: I never get a break.**
Therapist: You haven't got many breaks so far.

Client: He never does what we tell him to.
Therapist: When you see him cooperate, you will know we've made progress.

Here's another list of some of the words and phrases that reflect this technique:

- Yet
- So far
- After
- When.

TRY IT! **Client: I can't assert myself. I get too nervous.**
Therapist:

Client: I get numb from the waist down when I start to have sex.
Therapist:

There seems to be some connection between the places we have disowned inside ourselves and the key to where we need to go.

—David Whyte

3. Spirituality and The Inclusive Self

For me, Inclusive Therapy is related to *spirituality*. I define spirituality as anything that leads us to connect to something more within and/or beyond ourselves.

Sometimes in life we live small, and lose the sense that there is more than our petty interests, our egos, or our own lives. Sometimes we go small within ourselves, losing touch with our bodies or our deeper selves. Sometimes we go small by disconnecting from others or from the world. And we can go small by separating from our connection to the universal power that glues our whole existence together.

In discussing the 3-D model, I suggested that the inclusive self has room for contradictions, polarities, pluralities, and opposites. I want to extend that discussion here to include the spiritual conception of the inclusive self.

It is challenging to discuss spirituality. Spirituality can be ineffable, mysterious, and hard to pin down—like nailing Jell-O to a tree. But I have found a way to approach spirituality that most people can understand. While categorizing spirituality, this approach leaves spirituality open enough to include its inherent complexity. So, here goes.

Spirituality, in my conception, is when people feel connected to something beyond their petty, little selves (or egos). Spirituality refers to what is beyond the "little self," the personality. Anything that gives one an experience of the "bigger self," or what is beyond the limited personality, can be a component of spirituality.

Dean Ornish has said:

> When I say spirituality, I don't necessarily mean religion; I mean whatever it is that helps you feel connected to something that is larger than yourself.

Much of the material in the previous chapters could be seen as spiritual, even though it looked like we were discussing solutions, possibilities, or inclusive language and methods. That's because, in Inclusive Therapy, we have a view that people are never as limited or small as they initially appear when we begin therapy. When we get hooked into that sense that people are so small, stuck, or limited, we have forgotten the larger realities or possibilities that are available. In this chapter, however, we will make this larger self, The Inclusive Self, more available through explicitly spiritual methods.

3.1   Connect to the body

HELP PEOPLE FIND A WAY TO CONNECT OR RECONNECT TO THEIR
BODIES.

Often, due to trauma or shame, people have neglected or disconnected from their bodies. In this world we are embodied.
Connecting deeply to the body can lead to a
more inclusive sense of self, as well as a
more expansive relation to the
world. Different people have different preferred modes of connecting. Some people prefer more
athletic pursuits like running,
weight training, or competitive
sports. Others prefer more
aesthetic pursuits like dancing.
Still others prefer more sensual
pursuits like gourmet eating, sex,
working with clay, or taking a bubble
bath.

Probably the simplest way to help people connect to their bodies is to ask them how they have connected
with their bodies in the past or how they typically get in touch
with their bodies. If they don't have a usual means, you can suggest some of the modes noted above.

Practice: Connecting to the body

Find a way to help people to become more embodied, i.e.,
more aware of and connected to their senses and their bodily

experience. This can either be a revisiting and reminder of previous strategies or working out some new ways to accomplish this bodily connection. Gestalt Therapy founder Fritz Perls used to instruct:

Lose your mind and come to your senses.

By this he meant that many people are so intellectualized they forget to pay attention to their sensual experience.

EXAMPLES   **Client: I was sexually abused and don't spend much time in my body. I'm always running into furniture. I don't seem to know where my body is.**
Therapist: Can you tell me about a time when you felt connected in a good way to your body?

Client: Since we broke up, I miss cuddling—the feeling of skin on skin.
Therapist: Do you ever get massages?

Perhaps the best way to develop this type of response is to ask people you know—friends, family, colleagues, or clients—what they typically do to connect with their bodies or what are their best moments in relation to their bodies are. Make a list of these things and have it available for clients who may not have a clue about how to connect with their bodies.

TRY IT!   Client: Since I gained so much weight, I don't even want to
               see my body in the mirror.
               Therapist:

               Client: I get numb from the waist down when I start to have
               sex.
               Therapist:

3.2 Connect to the deeper self, the soul, or the spirit

HELP PEOPLE FIND A WAY TO CONNECT OR RECONNECT TO THEIR DEEPEST SENSE OF THEMSELVES OR THE WISDOM WITHIN.

When I studied with Milton Erickson, I discovered he didn't care much for religion. He would not use words like *soul* or *spirit*. Yet he had an almost religious faith in the wisdom we each carry deep inside. He called it the *unconscious mind:*

Trust your unconscious.

He would intone:

It knows more than you do.

To me, that was his code word for *soul*, although he couldn't bring himself to utter that word.

What I am referring to here is something beyond what the rational, logical mind has worked out. It suggests the accumulation of a lifetime of learning and observation. Yet, perhaps it is the wisdom we enter this life with—some little children seem like old souls to me; they seem to have a wisdom beyond their years.

Again, people have various ways of tapping into this deep wisdom. The best procedure is usually to ask them about their preferred modes of doing so. If they haven't got any in place, you might suggest meditation, journaling, sitting silently, paying attention to their breath-

ing, a retreat, or some other way that people use to get back in touch with their deeper selves.

Practice: Connecting to the deeper self, the soul or the spirit

Help people find a way to navigate the road to their deepest wisdom and intuitive knowledge of themselves.

EXAMPLES   **Client: When someone asks me to do something, my knee jerk reaction is to say "yes" to accommodate them. I usually can't tell whether it is right for me until later, when I have a chance to think about it and get in touch with what it true for me.**

Therapist: I had a similar pattern. I learned to say to people, "Let me sleep on it before I give you an answer." Somehow, even when I didn't think about it a lot, by the next day, I would usually have my answer. Do you think something like that would work for you?

Client: I can't remember why I chose this line of work. I'm so burned out.

Therapist: What do you typically do to get in touch with your deep inner self when you are feeling disconnected? Do you meditate, journal, go for a walk, or something else?

Again, one of the best ways to learn this technique is to ask people you know—friends, family, colleagues, or  clients—what they typically do to connect with themselves in a deep way. Also, ask yourself what do *you* typically do to connect with your inner wisdom? Make a list of these things and have it available for clients who may not have a clue about how to connect with their inner selves or spirits.

TRY IT!   **Client: I don't know what to do.**
               Therapist:

               Client: I'm thinking of going back to graduate school, but I
                   am not sure it is the right move.
               Therapist:

3.3   Connect to another being

HELP PEOPLE CONNECT OR RECONNECT TO A BEING DEEPLY AND
PROFOUNDLY.

I remember when my son was born, being there at his birth, I
had a profound sense of connection. Over the next week, I had
a series of perplexing images and fantasies. In these fantasies,
someone was attacking my wife and son, and I was defending
them, sometimes to the death. This was a bit disturbing to me.
I'm a peaceful guy and not prone to such images. Yet here I was
having them right after my child was born. Finally, I got the
message: *I would die for this little guy.* I was now living for someone other than myself.

Most of us have this experience at some time in our lives. We
connect deeply with a parent, a child, a friend, a teacher, a
mentor, or someone else. This connects us to something
beyond us.

I used to call this technique connecting to another *person* until
I had a client who stayed alive, although feeling suicidal, because
she wasn't willing to leave her dog; her only deep connection
was to an animal. I have found that other people have such a

deep connection with their horse or another animal, so I have revised the description of this pathway from connection to another *person* to connection to another *being*.

Practice: Connecting to another being

Finding or helping people create deep connections to at least one other person or animal.

EXAMPLES   **Client: I feel so alone.**

Therapist: Is there someone with whom you connect very deeply? Or someone you used to connect with like that? If they were here right now, what do you think they would say to you or do having heard you say that?

Client: I am so ashamed of what I am feeling.

Therapist: Is there someone whom you know would accept you no matter what you were feeling?

Ask your clients if there is any being, past or present, with whom they feel or have felt a deep connection. Sometimes you can have them literally contact that person or animal during moments of struggle or disconnection. Other times, it might be more workable or useful to have them imagine the person or animal is there for them at that moment.

TRY IT!   **Client:** I feel like a failure.

          Therapist:

          Client: I don't think anyone can accept me the way I am.

          Therapist:

Theory Break: Seven Pathways to Spirituality Through Connection

I think that there are seven pathways by which people connect to something bigger in their lives. The interesting part about some of these pathways is that they do not seem religious. Many people would not even consider them to be spiritual. So even people who have experienced religious trauma or those who think that spirituality is all New-Age claptrap can relate to one or more of these pathways.

1.   *Connection to the body.* This may come through dancing, sex, athletics, yoga, eating fine foods, and so on. Seeing Michael Jordan in the air about to make a basket or witnessing other great athletes in action can show the spiritual through the body—they seem to do things that are beyond usual human abilities and that seem transcendent.

2.   *Connection to the soul, the deeper self, the spirit.* This involves having a connection with oneself that is beyond the rational, the logical, or even the emotional. This is the deepest level within. Many people find that meditating, journaling, or just spending time alone helps them find this connection.

3. *Connection to another being.* This refers to intimate one-to-one relation-
    ships. Martin Buber calls this the I-Thou relationship. This pathway does
    not always need to refer to a relationship with another person; it could
    be with an animal. For example, I once had a client who was suicidal and
    the only thing that kept her alive for a time was her connection with
    her dog.

4. *Connection to community.* This pathway involves one's relationship to
    one's group, causes greater than oneself that contribute to the commu-
    nity, or the planet. If you have ever felt part of a family, extended family
    group, neighborhood, church group, or workplace, you have taken this
    pathway.

5. *Connection to nature.* This involves being in and noticing nature and the
    physical environment. How many of us need to spend time in the out-
    doors every so often so we do not begin to feel small and discon-
    nected? ("I believe in God, only I spell it Nature," said Frank Lloyd
    Wright.) One may also experience this sense of connection through a
    deep understanding and appreciation of the laws of nature, such as

those exhibited in physics. Being a liberal arts major, however, I think I'll stick with mountains, forests, and lakes for my nature connection.

6. *Connection by participating in making or by appreciating art.* Ever seen someone standing in front of a painting in a museum and being moved to tears? Or have you ever witnessed someone listening to a piece of music and feeling energized or moved? Depending on one's preferences, this connection may come through literature, painting, sculpture, theater, movies, photography, or dance. Many artists attest to a sense that they are not making the art they produce; it is coming to or through them.

7. *Connection to the Universe, higher power, God, cosmic consciousness.* You can substitute whatever word you prefer for the sense that there is a greater being or intelligence than ourselves at work in life. This connection can happen, for example, through prayer, meditating, or conversion to a religion. I once read a story in which a chronic alcoholic in therapy with Carl Jung begged for help. Jung replied that therapy had no help for his condition and he had never seen someone improve through therapy. When the man replied that this information didn't give him any hope, Jung agreed and said that the only thing he had ever seen make a difference in these situation was being converted to a religion. The man said that didn't offer much hope either. How was he supposed to get converted? Jung said that if it were him, he would attend every revival meeting he could find, regardless of denomination, and then hope one took. It actually worked. This advice, indirectly led to the founding of AA.

In the applied methods featured in this chapter, I address these pathways and offer some more detail on ways to help people connect to their bigger, inclusive selves through each of these pathways.

3.4 Connect to a group or community

HELP PEOPLE FIND SOME GROUP OF PEOPLE OR INSTITUTION WITH
WHICH THEY CAN IDENTIFY AND TO WHICH THEY CAN FEEL THEY
BELONG.

This connection is similar to the last one. In this case the technique directs clients toward groups like family, friends, church or neighborhood communities, internet communities, the people with whom they work—in short, any group of people with whom clients feel deeply connected. This connection draws clients beyond their isolated sense of identity.

Again, you might construct a list of ways in which your friends or your client connect to groups or organizations.

Practice: Connecting to a group or community

Find a way to connect people to groups like nuclear or extended families, interest groups, or colleagues.

EXAMPLES   **Client: I feel so alone.**

Therapist: Is there some group that you have thought about joining, like a church, a volunteer group, or some interest group?

Client: I am so ashamed of what I am feeling.

Therapist: There is a support group for people who have experienced sexual abuse that you might find helpful.

Ask your clients if there is any group of people or organization
with which they feel a strong connection. Then try to link them
to that group or, at least, the sense they get while connected
to that group. This might help solve their problems.

TRY IT!   **Client: I just sit around all day and smoke dope. Life just
        doesn't seem to interest me.**
        Therapist:

        **Client: I don't think anyone can understand what it is like to
        lose your child.**
        Therapist:

3.5   Connect to nature

HELP PEOPLE CONNECT OR RECONNECT TO THEIR NATURAL ENVI-
RONMENT OR THE WORLD IN SOME WAY.

There is some evidence that having a
view of nature helps people be
more productive at work, have
fewer days of absence or illness, and so on. There is also
evidence that having access to
a window that looks out on
nature can reduce boredom
and enhance creativity and help
post-operative healing.[*] In our
modern lives, however, we spend much of
our time in buildings without windows, out of touch with
nature.

A colleague of mine, George Burns, has even written a book
called *Nature-Guided Therapy*, in which he details all the evidence and ways in which nature can help solve therapeutic
problems. He suggests that couples having problems take a
walk in a nature setting to discuss their problems and finds
they often have better conversations in such settings.

---

* See N. J. Stone and J. M. Irvine (1994). Direct and indirect window access, task, type and per-
formance. *Journal of Environmental Psychology,* 14 (1): 57–63, as well as R. S. Ulrich (1984). View
through a window may influence recovery from surgery. *Science,* 224: 420–421.

Practice: Connecting to nature

Suggest to people that they spend time in a natural setting, especially when they are stressed or trying to resolve problems.

EXAMPLES   **Client: We're arguing almost every night.**

Therapist: I suggest the next time you are going to start a discussion you drive out of the city a short ways and take a walk in the woods. Walk in silence for a time and then begin your discussion.

Client: I am so ashamed of what I am feeling.

Therapist: Is there any place out in nature in which you feel really peaceful and okay?

Can you find some way (again either from clients' histories or by creating some new ways) of connecting people to nature? They might take a walk, visit the mountains, take a trip to the ocean, take up gardening, or do anything else that brings them into contact with the natural world.

TRY IT!   **Client:** I feel like a failure.

          Therapist:

          Client: I don't think anyone can accept me the way I am.

          Therapist:

3.6   Connect through art

HELPING PEOPLE CONNECT OR RECONNECT BY EITHER CREATING
ART OR WITNESSING ART.

I was reading a book full of interviews with singer-songwriters.
What struck me as I read the interviews was how many of the
songwriters spoke about the experience that the songs they
wrote "came though them." It was, by their accounts, almost as
if the music were dictated from beyond them. The best art
seems to have this transcendent quality.

This applied method involves helping people discover or redis-
cover art in some way. Some people already have or have had
an artistic or creative pursuit that provides this connection.
Others just like to participate in art as a reader, viewer, or listener. Anything that involves people in art in a way that
expands their selves and connects them with the larger world
fits with this approach.

Practice: Connecting through art

Encourage people to tell you what artistic pursuits they have
enjoyed and help them reconnect with those, especially around
the problem they are dealing with.

EXAMPLES   **Client: Nobody understands me.**

**Therapist: Is there a particular song that
you think would help me get a
sense of who you are?**

Client: I am so ashamed of what I am feeling.

Therapist: You said you really feel creative and connected when you draw. Can you draw me a picture of that shame?

List some typical art activities that people you know do or participate in. Find out if clients like any of these or any other art activities. Find a way to connect them to art in relation to their therapeutic problems.

TRY IT!   Client: I feel like a failure.

Therapist:

Client: I am constantly checking to see whether I have turned off the stove when I have left the house. Sometimes I go back three or four times after I have left, even though I have already checked.

Therapist:

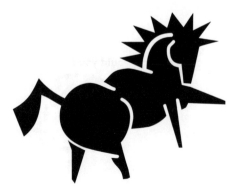

3.7 Connect to God, the universe, a Higher Power, or some other transcendent being

HELP PEOPLE CONNECT OR RECONNECT TO SOME BEING OR FORCE BEYOND THEMSELVES, BEYOND PEOPLE, AND BEYOND THIS WORLD.

Many religions have traditions, narratives, and symbols that help connect people to a supreme being or transcendent entity of some kind (commonly called *God*). I usually search in three directions for this element: the past, the present, and the future.

The Past

Have you ever had any religious beliefs or practices?
How were those beliefs or practices helpful for you?

The Present

Is there any spiritual figure or activity that you think would be helpful for you in this situation?
If you could write a prayer right now, what would it be?

The Future

What kind of spiritual activities, if any, would you like to do in the future?
Is there any area of your spiritual life you would like to develop?
Is there any spiritual figure that you would like to use as a model for you? In what way?

Practice: Connecting to God, the universe, a Higher Power, or some other transcendent being

Find any place in which clients feel connected to something bigger, beyond the human. Then find out if they can use that bigger sense of things as a source to tap into for solutions to their problems.

EXAMPLES **Client: I am afraid to die.**

Therapist: Do you have any sense that there is a force beyond the human? Have you ever had this sense? If so, could that be useful for you right now as you face death?

Client: I'm not sure what I am living for.

Therapist: Do you think we are just random balls of DNA thrown onto this planet or do you think we are here for a purpose?

Obviously, if clients have already brought up their religious or spiritual beliefs, then you can easily use this aspect of their lives. If they haven't, start much more vaguely. Use words and phrases like, *force beyond people, higher power, guiding intelligence,* or some such notion before using the *G* word. Talk of God might put some people off.

TRY IT!   **Client:** I feel like a failure.

              Therapist:

              Client: I can't figure out what I am supposed to do with my
                   life.

              Therapist:

It's not enough to hate your enemy. You have to understand how you bring each other to a deep completion.

—Don DeLillo

4. Bigotry: Using Inclusion to Deal with Internal and External Conflicts

I went to a workshop on racism some time ago in which the presenters divided us into groups. One group was put on one side of a line and the other group was put on the other side. The group I was in was privately told to see the other group as having bad or undesirable qualities: for example, they were variously shifty, stupid, lazy, mean, evil, drunks, criminals, or drug addicts. The other group was given similar instructions about my group. Then we were told to interact with each other. As you might imagine, there were conflicts and misunderstandings. Generally, we found that we clustered with "our" groups and preferred to interact within "our" groups. We generally began to see all the "others" as negative in some way. We either avoided the "others" or felt some level of alienation or hostility toward "them." Even though this was only an exercise, and the groups were randomly created, we sought

out and felt more akin to members of "our" artificially created groups.

One of the keys to racism is seeing someone else as the "other"—essentially separate and distant from one or one's group. Another key is the attribution of negative traits to the "other." And a third element is generalization: We tend to see all or none; rather than individuals, we see stereotypes. In racism we miss the various shades of gray and see only black or white (sometimes literally, of course).

When the other is defined negatively, we have one of two typical responses.

- We withdraw or avoid.
- We want to get rid of or kill off the other.

In the first response, we do an inner ethnic cleansing. (Remember our conception of inhibition or numbing in the discussion of the 3-D Model.) In the second, we project the things we find unacceptable, bad, and evil outward, and begin to do outer ethnic cleansing.

I once had a phone consultation with a couple, Petra and Sam, that was having major conflicts. They would argue, close to the point of violence; and they did this on a regular basis. A friend of mine, Warren, was doing marital therapy with them and, although he was usually very good with couples, Warren found them too intractable. He suggested they have a phone consultation with me to see if I could help them get unstuck. Petra and Sam

were very distrustful of one another. Anything the one did was immediately pounced upon by the other, as badly intentioned, and then they were off to the races as mutual recriminations lead to heightening anger. They were both angry with one another and yet somehow hooked so deeply they couldn't break up.

I was able to help Petra and Sam somewhat. Each began to be less suspicious of the other's motives and they stopped triggering each other to anger so often. After several consultations over the course of a few months, Petra and Sam were arguing less and feeling more neutral (rather than angry) toward one another. They had also been able to resolve several long-standing  conflicts. But I could never get them much past neutral. Petra and Sam had decided to stay together but there wasn't much love or affection between them. Mutually we decided that they had gotten all they could from me and we parted ways.

About six months later, the couple contacted me. Petra and Sam told me they were now feeling very deeply connected and in love, and they thanked me for the crucial help I had given them. I was curious about what brought about such a dramatic change. Petra and Sam told me they had attended a Harville Hendrix seminar in their town and had received one very valuable insight.

The insight Petra and Sam got was this:

**When your partner does something that upsets you, it is a
clue that whatever he or she has done has touched upon
some unfinished or unincorporated aspect of
yourself.**

This unincorporated aspect might be an
unfinished issue, an old trauma related
to one of your parents, or a
message that there is
some part of you
that you do not
accept. In any case,
instead of just getting
upset and reacting,
Hendrix had some proce-
dures to help couples use these
upsets as cues for engaging in per-
sonal work. He invited partners to
soften and be more compassionate
when their partner became triggered.
Petra and Sam instantly realized how true this was for them
and took it to heart. Since the Hendrix seminar, they had been
softer with one another at those moments of upset. They had
even begun to thank each other every time they got upset,
because their partner had now given them an opportunity to
resolve some unfinished issue within them. This had led to profound feelings of closeness and love.

Now, without wanting to be disrespectful of Hendrix, who has
contributed much to couples all over the world, I submit that

the idea that had so moved this couple is not *the* truth—it is merely a hypothesis. And just because it may hold true for a particular couple, it certainly doesn't follow that it is universally true for all couples or is applicable to every upsetting incident. But it had a favorable effect with Petra and Sam in that it helped them be more compassionate toward one another, especially at moments that were most challenging and previously likely to lead to anger and non-compassion.

In this chapter, I provide a few inclusive applied methods geared toward softening one's attitude toward oneself and others. These techniques can help one become more accepting and compassionate toward those aspects of oneself or others that have been defined negatively as "bad."

4.1   Elicit self-compassion

FIND A WAY TO HELP PEOPLE SOFTEN AND BECOME MORE ACCEPT-
ING, LESS JUDGMENTAL TOWARD THEMSELVES.

People are often self-critical or treat themselves harshly. One
of the things we can do as therapists is to help them soften
toward themselves, become less self-judgmental and more self-
accepting.

Practice: Eliciting self-compassion

There are some contexts and ways of thinking that are more
compassionate that I think are available to all clients. Find a
way to tap into those contexts and points of view to help people soften toward themselves. For example, they might be able
to recall a time when they felt some sympathy toward someone they had not previously understood or with whom they
had not sympathized. They might be able to recall a time when
they felt patient toward a child who did something that wasn't
right because the child did not know he or she was doing
something wrong.

EXAMPLES   Client: I'm so stupid. I keep messing up.

Therapist: Have you ever heard the saying, "Be patient with
me, God's not finished with me yet"? It sounds like God's
not finished with you. You're still learning. And making
mistakes is one of
the ways we learn.

Client: I just hate myself.

Therapist: If your grandmother, who you said always loved you and was kind to you, were here right now, how do you think she would see you?

Often I ask people how they are seen by others—friends or family—who love them. Or I ask them how they would view those same people if they had done the same things for which they are so critical of themselves. If their friends were to know about the things they think are so unacceptable about themselves, what would the friends say in response? Or if their beloved friend or child were thinking such things about themselves, what would the client say to the friend or child?

TRY IT!   Client: Since I gained so much weight, I don't even want to see my body in the mirror.

Therapist:

Client: I get numb from the waist down when I start to have sex.

Therapist:

4.2   Elicit compassion for others

FIND A WAY TO HELP PEOPLE SOFTEN AND BECOME MORE ACCEPTING
AND LESS JUDGMENTAL OF OTHERS.

Sometimes finding a way to empathize with others or, at least,
to blame them less can reduce anger or conflict. It may also
provide a way of being less
critical and more accepting of
oneself and aspects of one's
own experience.

Anne McCaffrey advised:

Make no judgments where you have no compassion.

We have all made mistakes and done things that are not so
smart or nice.

I heard a story about two great social scientists meeting one
day after many years of merely knowing
about each others' work from publications
and conference papers. These were great
intellects. They met outside a conference
and sat down together while taking a break
from the sessions. When someone later asked what they had
talked about, one of the famous social scientists replied:

> We agreed that, from all that we had learned and
> observed, sometimes human being treat each other
> worse than dogs. And that it would be good if we could
> all be a little nicer to one another.

The listener was astonished that these great minds had come to such a simple notion, but I find it very profound indeed.

Compassion is not forgiveness. Nor does it involve excusing other people's harmful or bad behavior. I am referring to a certain softening toward others and a recognition of the humanness of us all.

Practice: Eliciting compassion for others

Tap into contexts or ways of thinking that naturally soften judgments toward others.

EXAMPLES   **Client: Why does he have to be so irresponsible? He pays bills late and then I get the consequences.**

Therapist: I suspect that approaching him in the way you are is just backing him further into the corner. Is there a way you could approach him with a bit more compassion for his flaws so you two could start working together on solving this bill-paying problem?

Client: So she gets anxious. Does that mean I have to listen to her whine when I'd rather be reading the paper?

Therapist: It sounds as if she's asking you to give up a bit of paper-reading time to help her calm down initially, as she has a lot of trouble doing that on her own. Then she would be more understanding of your wanting space-out and reading time.

Here are some areas to examine and specific questions to consider regarding compassion:

Does your life exhibit an atmosphere of compassion? Or are you more judgmental and harsh?

How could you create or enhance an atmosphere of compassion and kindness in your life?

If this person were your child or best friend, how would you view them or relate to him or her?

Think of the most serene, compassionate, or wise person you know. How would he or she view this situation or deal with it?

Remember a time when you were judgmental or critical of someone, and then softened your attitude and became more compassionate. How did you make that shift? What changed after you made that shift? Can you apply any of that to your current situation?

TRY IT!   Client: She's overweight and I just don't feel sexually attracted to her anymore.
Therapist:

Client: He refuses to confront his mother. She criticizes everyone and he just lets her get away with it.
Therapist:

Under the most rigorously
controlled conditions of pressure,
temperature, volume, humidity, and
other variables, the organism will
do as it damn well pleases.
—The Harvard Law

5. The Inclusive Therapist, or I'm Sorry, but My Karma Just Ran over Your Dogma

Here's where things get really interesting. This inclusive stuff isn't just for clients. If one takes these inclusive ideas seriously, they challenge the therapist's rigidities, precious beliefs, and preferred methods.

Because I was trained as a family/systemic therapist in the early, evangelical years of the movement (the mid-1970s), I considered medications, diagnosis, and psychodynamic therapies as the evil empires. As the years went on, though, I occasionally saw someone get so much more benefit from taking medications than the best I had to offer as a therapist. As a result, I mellowed. Yes, perhaps medication is used too often, but it is sometimes very helpful. I have also become friends with some of those "evil" psychodynamic therapists over the years and have found them to be caring, intelligent, and well-intentioned people who have sometimes helped people in ways I couldn't. Some of my clients have shown me that receiving a diagnosis has been such a relief and so validating of their experience that

I have given up my blanket opposition to the practice. It is also helpful for insurance reimbursement, I have discovered.

I once asked the English anthropologist/biologist Gregory Bateson what he thought about Richard Bandler and John Grinder's notion of people being either primarily visual, auditory, or kinesthetic. (I was enamored of the idea at that time.) Gregory told me that he had at first been enormously impressed with the idea. But then, he said, he found it too rigid. "All typologies," Gregory intoned in his deep British accent, "if held too tightly, become pathologies." The Milan Associates used to say:

Don't marry your hypotheses.

I have the sense that we therapists had better be careful even going out on dates with our hypotheses, since we get attached to them rather quickly.

We tell our clients or patients things with a tone of certainty:

Your depression is biochemical and you will have to be on medication the rest of your life.
Your problem is your issues with your family of origin.
It took a long time to develop this problem and it will take a long time to resolve it.

We must remember that these are *only ideas which may be helpful,* but also may not be helpful in particular situations with particular people.

As psychologist/family therapist Alan Gurman once said:

Our first loyalty should be to our clients, not our theories.

Beware of what I call *theory counter-transference,* a process in which you unwittingly transfer your theories to your clients and they begin to live your ideas.

The point is that while I still have preferred theories, methods, and ideas, these are continually challenged by my willingness to recognize and include the complex reality of therapy, my clients, and life.

This quotation from Emile Chartier is to the point:

There is nothing as dangerous as an idea when it is the only one you have.

So, when you are an inclusive therapist, you may have to give up your cherished beliefs and dogmas in favor of noticing what is actually helpful and responding to the particular people with whom you are working.

The important thing is to not stop questioning.

—Albert Einstein

6. Or Not: An Envoi

I couldn't, in good conscience, leave you without a word of warning, which I think you'll understand and appreciate now that you've read this book.

Nothing I have told you in this book is true.

That is, all I have given you is a series of ideas and techniques that I think are useful.

Human beings are much more complex than our theories, methods, and words. After being a therapist for more than 28 years, I am continually humbled when I recognize how much *we don't know* about the change process. I am also humbled when I think of how flexible and willing to learn we must be in order to be of service to the people  who seek our help when they are suffering or concerned about their lives or their loved ones.

So remember:

Be inclusive, except when you aren't.
Be flexible, except when that doesn't work.

I think what I have said in this book is valuable, but only when it is held very lightly.

Bill O'Hanlon writes books and teachers workshops around the world. He prefers, however, to hang out with his wife and son, to play lots of music, to read books, and to watch movies. This is his 20th book (stop him before he writes again!). His biggest claims to fame, however, are that he was once on Oprah and Clint Black wrote a country song inspired by one of his books. Contact Bill at PossiBill@aol.com or visit his Web site www.brieftherapy.com.